THE
MIS-EDUCATION
OF BLACK YOUTH
IN AMERICA

ettelloc Publishing
734 Franklin Avenue
Suite 235
Garden City, NY 11530
www.ettellocPublishing.com

Printed in the United States of America
First Printing, 2015
ISBN-13: 978-0-9898304-3-0
ISBN-10: 0-9898304-3-8
LCCN: 2015947731

Wallace, Rick, 1967- author.
The mis-education of black youth in America:
the final move on the grand chessboard / Rick Wallace.
pages cm
Includes bibliographical references.
LCCN 2015947731
ISBN 9780989830430

1. African American youth--Education. 2. African
American youth--Social conditions. 3. United States--
Race relations. I. Title.

LC2717.W35 2015   371.829'96073
QBI15-600189

THE MIS-EDUCATION OF BLACK YOUTH IN AMERICA

THE FINAL MOVE ON THE GRAND CHESSBOARD

RICK WALLACE
PH.D.

Ettelloc Publishing
NY

CONTENTS

Glossary of Uncommon Words

There is a vital element of writing that I am constantly thinking about, and that is our purpose for writing. This is an element that I find myself in constant conflict with, primarily due to the fact that I refuse to dumb down my writing style because there may be word usage uncommon to the average reader. This stance normally places me at odds with content editors and publishers; however, very rarely am I overruled on word usage.

It is important to understand that my vernacular is not meant to be condescending, but it is my active vocabulary, which allows me to effectively communicate the message that I am attempting to deliver. I believe that the ability to communicate through a broad vocabulary carries with it great power to control one's destiny. Far too many times I have witnessed my black brothers and sisters stand in the right, but not be able to effectively communicate their feelings or a particular situation, which then leads to an unfavorable outcome. When I speak or write, I challenge those who will read or hear me to increase their active vocabulary.

I am a firm believer that any person has the capacity to improve their vocabulary, but if a person is never challenged to raise their manner of expression, they will not. With that being said, I did not alter my writing style in the slightest; however, I have created an in-flow glossary of uncommon words. This means that words that may be considered uncommon will be footnoted with a brief definition of the word, meaning that the reader will be able to scan the bottom of the page to discover the meaning of uncommon words. If for some reason you come across a word that you don't recognize, take the time to look up the definition and familiarize yourself with the word. You will thank me for it later. Happy reading.

Introduction

When AO Green and Ettelloc Publishing approached me with the idea of writing a book on the mis-education of black youth in America, I thought it was an exceptional idea. I had conducted hours of research, and I had written a number of short treatises on the topic; however, I had never endeavored to address the issue in a more comprehensive manner. My initial postulation[1] was that it would be an easy endeavor, being that I had compiled the majority of the data that would be necessary to write the book, but the more that I began to peel back the layers of this enigmatic[2] issue, the more I realized just how complex the dynamic of the mis-education of black youth is.

From a superficial perspective, one can examine the fact that young black children are under-educated as they progress through a European-based educational program, but a more in depth examination of the process unveils a number of systematic occurrences that go far beyond the simple failure of the public education system in this country. I immediately found myself faced with the challenge of painting a detailed portrait of white supremacy racism and the substantial role that it plays in the mis-education of black youth and blacks in general.

As I began to unravel this web of treachery, it became almost overwhelming at the lengths that white supremacy has gone in order to ensure that the white elite would maintain their positions of power

---

[1] Postulate: to assume or claim as true, existent, or necessary.

[2] Enigmatic: of, relating to, or resembling an enigma; mysterious.

and dominance—not only in America, but globally. There are multitudinous[3] machinations[4] through which white supremacy has carried out its successful campaign to oppress African Americans; however, there are very few adverse mechanisms that have the complexity that the system of mis-education has. It is also important to understand that the mis-education of black youth extends beyond the corridors of American schools and invades almost every facet of black culture, including entertainment mediums such as television and music.

The correlation between the disproportionate rates of young black boys being diagnosed with learning and behavioral disorders such as ADHD, mental retardation, learning disabled, oppositional defiant disorder and more, and the Private Prison Industrial Complex is especially disturbing. There is a lucid and inextricable[5] connection between the manner in which our young black boys are treated in the early stages of the educational process and the establishment of a school-to-prison pipeline that leads from the back doors or schools to the front doors of prisons. The complexity and devastation of this one simple element of the greater scheme is worthy of its own volume; nonetheless, I dedicate a significant part of the book to unveiling this vile attempt to destroy the black male by any means necessary.

THE AFRICAN AMERICAN PSYCHE

One of the challenges that the African American community faces is their limited perspicacity[6] of the psychological impact of slavery and the subsequent institutional, governmental and social mechanisms

---

[3] Multitudinous: innumerable, of a multitude, many.

[4] Machinations: schemes, plots, maneuverings.

[5] Inextricable: forming a maze of tangle from which it is impossible to get free.

[6] Perspicacity: perceptiveness, understanding, discernment.

that have negatively impacted the black self-image. It is imperative that blacks understand why they think and behave in the manner that they do. It is immensely important to understand that a significant amount of blacks are suffering from a diminished self-image that has the capacity to feed self-hatred. How blacks view work, property and personal business opportunities is a direct result of chattel slavery and the subsequent institutions that followed. Both, Dr. Na'im Akbar and Dr. Joy DeGruy, refer to this form of psychosis as Post Traumatic Slave Syndrome—describing a set of specific beliefs, behaviors and actions that are directly associated with the multigenerational trauma that has been experienced by African Americans at the hands of their white oppressors.

It is important to gain a lucid apprehension of this particular psychological development within the black psyche, because it directly impacts the capacity for blacks to effectively march out of their valley of oppression. PTSS should not be viewed as an excuse for substandard behavior or mediocre accomplishments, but as a basis for understanding the current plight of blacks, and subsequently developing an efficacious[7] plan of action that will help to ignite an evolution of the black psyche—subsequently resulting in an evolution of the black race.

It is also important because it is the education system in America that is used as an element of reinforcement of the social norms that have established the erroneous paradigms that suggest that blacks are inferior to whites and incapable of achieving greatness on a collective scale. Until blacks are able to evolve in their collective psyche to a position in which they have a heightened sense of self-awareness,

---

[7] Efficacious: having the power to produce a desired result.

no grand scheme dedicated to black empowerment will ever gain traction. An authentic movement is built upon the belief and hope of something better or greater, but as long as a substantial amount of blacks believe that substandard living is their lot in life, it will be virtually impossible to enlist them into the struggle of upward mobility.

AN IDENTITY CRISIS

Over 300 years of chattel slavery and another 150 years of oppressive measures by white supremacy America has effectively robbed blacks of their identity and self-awareness. Without self-consciousness, it is impossible for blacks to achieve any level of aggregate[8] success in America. As long as the black man views the white man as superior and the white system of achievement as something to aspire to, he will be restricted in his mobility. Because proper education is the process of creating self-consciousness on multiple levels, the mis-education of the black youth in American serves to further exacerbate the generational perpetuation of a poor self-image.

Although self-awareness is more than the existence of information, information is an integral part of the process of self-awareness, meaning that when so much of a young black boy or girl's history is withheld from them, they will never be able to develop a healthy self-image.

STILL NOT FREE

It was Thomas Jefferson that once stated, "It is impossible to be ignorant and free." It is on this premise that I strongly suggest that American slavery never actually ended, but the mechanism of slav-

---

[8] Aggregate: formed by the collection of units or particles into a body, mass, or amount; collective.

ery shifted from one of physical chattel slavery to that of mental or psychological slavery. If ignorance is an inhibiting factor in the quest for freedom, then blacks are still bound to a substandard life—not by physical chains, but by the psychological chains that are manufactured through the ignorance of self.

It is incumbent upon every black parent and resident of this nation to seize every opportunity to enlighten our youth as it pertains to their identity and heritage. We must come to a point of understanding that it is quite foolish to expect the oppressor to provide the fruit of freedom. Those who know the truth have an inherent responsibility to share their knowledge with those who are yet consumed by the pernicious force of ignorance.

This book not only addresses the challenges that are associated with the mis-education of our youth, but it presents some short-term and long-term solutions that must be implemented if we are to ever truly realize our greatness as a people.

DEFINING WHITE SUPREMACY RACISM

The truth is that if most people in America were surveyed, regardless of race, the vast majority would not have sufficient perspicacity of what racism actually is. Most people confuse bigotry with racism. This is why it is so easy for whites to accuse blacks of reverse racism—one of the most effective countermeasures to arguments of blacks against white supremacy. This is why it is paramount that blacks gain an understanding of what genuine racism is.

Racism is not bigotry or hatred of another race, although bigotry and hatred may very well be present in the execution of certain mechanisms of white supremacy racism. First, let's take a brief look at a functional definition of racism: "White supremacy racism is a historically based, institutionally perpetuated system of exploitation and oppression of continents, nations, and peoples of color by white people and nations of the European continent, for the purpose of maintaining and defending a system of wealth, power, and privilege."[9]

What is important to understand in this definition is the presence of a system of power. Racism does not exist without a system of power that has the capacity to negatively impact a group of people on a collective level. Although there are blacks that may have a strong disdain for whites, the absence of any institutional power source through which they can negatively impact whites collectively, eliminates the argument of reverse racism. Hatred and bigotry are an issue; however, racism is something completely different.

Seeing racism as a power system is immensely important to understanding the motive, intent and devastating implications associated with the mis-education of black youth. One of the gravest mistakes that we make as blacks is in our perception of racism as a collection of individual acts of discrimination and prejudices perpetuated against blacks. Failure to acknowledge the systematic formulation and execution of actions and activities that effectively create an entire culture of subjugation is what makes this battle so futile for blacks at this point.

White supremacy is not executed by rednecks in the hills of Tennessee and Kentucky—although they serve a purpose within the system—it is the institutionally facilitated propaganda campaigns that effectively disseminate the message that convinces these individuals that they are superior to blacks. That is what represents the system of racism. Racism is played out in government, politics, financial insti-

---

[9] Elizabeth Martinez, "What is White Supremacy?" *SOA Watch: Close the School of the Americas*, http://soaw.org/index.php?option=com_content&view=article&id=482 (accessed June 10, 2014).

tutions, educational systems and every other facet of society. It is the collective machine that drives the mindset and activities of the masses. As a system, racism effectively impacts every aspect of existence of this country.

The system has been designed to invade and influence all nine areas of human activity which are economics, education, entertainment, labor, law, politics, religion, sex and war.[10] The systematic flow of white supremacy is highly cohesive and focused. The system is functioning at an optimal level, even when there are no blatant acts of racism visible. It is pervasive in the TV shows we watch, the text books our children read, the marketing content shared by corporations, etc.

When blacks fail to view racism as a systemic issue, it leads to the personalization of racist acts, making us vulnerable to the rebuttal of reverse racism, and the "not all whites are racist argument." When racism is seen as a system, it is much easier to discern the motivation and intent of the poisonous system. Using the term "supremacy" helps to define the power relationship that is necessary to carry out the tenets of genuine racism. The use of the term "supremacy" in no ways suggests that white people are supreme or superior to blacks. It simply provides context that elucidates the function and intent of the white racist system in play.

So, when we examine the devastating effects that the mis-education of our youth is having on us as a whole, we must do so with the understanding of the role that white supremacy Racism is playing in this dynamic—removing any postulations that this is simply a collective of isolated events. The mis-education of our youth is no accident. It is the result of precise efforts taken to ensure that the

---

[10] Francis Cress-Welsing, *The Cress Theory of Color Confrontation* (Washington, DC: C-R Publishers, 1989).

black race remains ignorant and complicit with the tenets of white supremacy.

THE GRAND CHESSBOARD

The phrase, "The Grand Chessboard," is used in the title of this book for a good reason. I have heard several of the great minds in the black community, including Dr. Claud Anderson, imply that blacks insist on playing checkers, while white supremacy America is playing chess. Although the boards are identical, the strategies are completely different. After reading *The Grand Chessboard* by Zbigniew Brzezinski, a major figure in the development of the updated infrastructure of white supremacy on a global scale, I became keenly cognizant[11] of the historical context of white supremacy and the model of domination that is being used to effectively oppress a specific group of people. It reminds me of the true nature of racism, which is not hatred, but absolute dominance. It is built on the foundational principle of self-preservation.

Chess is a game of strategy, and each dominant chess master has developed their own unique strategy for effectively dominating their opponent. There are some chess masters who are extremely aggressive, strategically attacking their opponent from multiple angles simultaneously. Although this strategy leaves the chess master vulnerable, they rarely pay the price, because their aggressive approach keeps their opponent on the defensive.

There are other chess masters that play a highly defensive game or a game of attrition. This strategy takes a great deal of patience, and the ability to decipher the strategy of the opponent, and over the course of the game the chess master simply outlasts their opponent.

---

[11] Cognizant: knowing, aware conscious.

When we make white supremacy racism analogous to *chess*, we are placing the system of white supremacy in the seat of the grand master, and blacks are currently at the mercy of an opponent who is more committed to a more defined strategy. The only hope for blacks on the grand chessboard is to recognize the strategy of our opponent, while simultaneously developing a progressive and lucid strategy of our own. The problem that we are facing now is that our current strategy of simply moving out of check will never net us a victory, and we will eventually find ourselves in checkmate—that situation from which we will not be able to recover.

It is my belief that the mis-education of black youth could very easily be the checkmate that I fear, and it is almost inevitable without immediate, responsive action by the black collective. The reason that the mis-education of black youth is so dangerous is the fact that it is multidimensional. This is a scheme that perpetuates the myth of black inferiority, leaving black youth with a mindset that perceives whites as superior. It is hard to prepare to compete with and defeat an opponent that you view as superior.

This system of mis-education also attacks the black male image in a number of ways, including the feminization and homosexualization of the black male image, the designation of learning disabilities as being inherent[12] to the black male, and the Private Prison Industrial Complex fed through the school to prison pipeline. If the black man is eliminated from the equation through these multiple mechanisms, the reproduction of the black race in America will be diminished to the point that the race will eventually die off. This is why I assert that the mis-education of our black youth could very well be the final

---

[12] Inherent: involved in the constitution or essential character of something or someone: belonging by nature or habit: intrinsic.

move on the grand cheboard. If we don't find a way to counter this move, we will find ourselves in checkmate.

Although this book is about the mis-education of back youth in America, you will discover a strong theme that examines the idea and concept of black group economics. It is important that these two themes, just as the black marriage, are not exclusive of one another. They are inextricably bound, for there is nothing that can be done to address the conundrum of the mis-education of black youth without the possession of economic influence and economic mobility. Make no mistake about it. The problem is the failure to adequately educate and empower our children on a holistic level; nevertheless, the solution is found in our ability to effectively mobilize and empower ourselves. There is no way around it.

EDUCATION

is the medium by which
a people are prepared for
the creation of their own
particular civilization,
and the advancement and
glory of their own race.

Marcus Garvey
*The Philosophy and Opinions
of Marcus Garvey
1923*

Chapter 1

Fading to Black

To effectively gain a lucid perspicacity of the devastating effects of the mis-education of a people, especially when it comes to its youth, we must take a look into the current state of affairs of blacks in America. By examining our current condition, we will be able to detect the systematic influence of white supremacy in the lives and culture of blacks in this country. As stated earlier, blacks tend to view the activity in this country on an individual and isolated basis, which limits our understanding of how the system is operating to maintain its control over them.

Racism must be viewed as a system and a bureaucracy, in that it is not only designed to invade and permeate every orifice of humanity on a global level, but it is also designed to be self-sustaining. What this means is that racism does not only protect the elite and powerful, but it inherently protects itself from being dismantled and rendered ineffective. Racism consistently searches for mechanisms that can be used to further oppress and control those whom it rules over. As we journey through this chapter, we will find that racism has impacted nearly every aspect of our lives, and the educational process is simply one of the more complex mechanisms through which it carries out its holistic assault on blacks.

ECONOMIC CASTRATION

Anyone who has followed me for any time understands the passion that I have for economic empowerment. The truth is that we as a people cannot truly achieve empowerment and elevation without first achieving collective economic empowerment[1]—through black group economics—practiced vertically. A brief examination of African American history reveals that economic impotence has been one of the greatest impediments of true black empowerment.

It is obvious that all of the ills associated with the mis-education of black youth can be identified, anatomized and the solution conceptually constructed; however, if the economic power that is necessary to institute changes is not present, it is all just a practice in futility. Throughout this book you will come in contact with the terms "economic empowerment" and "black group economics," so it is important to present a basic example of how group economics works in the black community, and how it is essential for creating the foundation upon which we will build our edifice of power, which will facilitate our ability to impact the education of our children and so much more. In this example, we will use the beauty supply industry—an industry in which blacks generate 96 percent of the revenue in a $15 billion per year industry.

HE WHO HAS THE GOLD MAKES THE RULES:
USING GROUP ECONOMICS TO DOMINATE THE BEAUTY SUPPLY INDUSTRY

A recent report revealed that the beauty supply industry is a $15

---

[1] Economic empowerment: the capacity to participate in, contribute to and benefit from financial growth processes in ways that recognize the value of the contributions being made, respects the dignity of the contributors and make it possible to negotiate a fairer distribution of the benefits of growth.

2

billion per year industry. Of this $15 billion, blacks generate 96 percent of the revenue. This means that $14.4 billion of the annual revenue generated in the beauty supply industry are black dollars. This lays the foundation for blacks to dominate the industry at every facet. Unfortunately, we are not even close to achieving this goal yet. We own less than three percent of the businesses in this industry.

I participated in a dialogue on this topic earlier today, and I decided to use the points I made then to present a picture to a much broader audience. One of the original concerns was that others already had the industry on lock. The truth is that the simple laws of economics are in the favor of blacks, if we choose to aggregate our spending power.

The simple rules of economics dictate that any industry dominated in patronage by a particular group can be dominated on the enterprise side of the spectrum of said group. Blacks generate $14.4 billion of this $15 billion industry, simple mathematics says that we (blacks) are the only ones that actually have the power to put the industry on lock—economics 101. We have the same influence in the seafood industry, where we outspend whites by $9 for every $1 dollar they spend. This means that our money sustains the industry, therefore we have the economic influence to take control over the enterprise side of the spectrum.

It has been suggested that we locked ourselves out of the industry after integration, because the vast majority of blacks would rather work for whites than maintain black-owned businesses. We did lock ourselves out of this industry, but the "key" is never any further than economic management. Again, if you sustain an industry with your money, you have the power to shift the control of that industry in your favor. Simply reinvesting in new black owned businesses at all

3

levels of the industry shifts the game—forcing non-black owners to at least partner with blacks. Now the door is open and the quest for domination begins.

The next question was centered on the fact that most pro-black supporters are anti-weave. Actually, as far as "weave" is concerned, although it makes up a significant portion of the revenue generated in the beauty supply industry, it is not the sole product that has substantial revenue generation potential, plus I don't think that the issue is extensions as much as it is against European-influenced extensions. There is an entire market for afrocentric extensions. Moreover, having ownership within the industry allows us to influence the culture, making European influence less impactful.

One of the first things that we have to stop doing is making excuses of why we can't do something. There is no such thing as can't. Recently, I saw a video of a man who was born with palsy and he could not control his movements and had no dexterity. Yet this man taught himself to draw using the top ten keys of a typewriter. The art is so detailed that it looks like portraits. Here we are allowing ourselves to be stumped by something as simple as where the hair originates. Once again, he who has the gold makes the rules. I believe $14.4 billion out of a $15 billion industry means that we have the gold. It is time that we start acting like it.

Throughout the conversation, there were those who seemed to be consistently focused on what they thought could not be done. Simply listening to a person in the midst of dialogue tells you a great deal about where a person is at and what they have done and are doing. The word *can't* flows too easily off the keyboard and lips of far too many blacks.

We are the people who built the pyramids, and yet we shrink back at the challenge of engaging an industry that would crumble if we pulled out our money. I will say this one more time. He who has the gold makes the rules. This principle is tens of thousands of years old and it has never failed. Stop saying can't and start asking how? That is exactly what they did when we turned away from the industry. And for the record, the current global economy does not freeze out group economics practiced vertically, but facilitates it. What you see with the three major automakers (Ford, GM and Chrysler) working together, is actually a form of group economics, which provides the stability and control over a particular market. This can be done by blacks in any industry in which our dollars sustain that industry.

To the question of how do we change the mindset of blacks who have done things the wrong way for so long, my answer was: We were infected with poor images, thinking and economic paradigms, so through the same mechanisms, such as media and education, we infect the minds of blacks. This infection will serve as an inoculation to the original infection and as a new infection within itself. The human mind is powerful, but it is immensely predictable. I would suggest reading the book *Propaganda* by Edward Berneys and *Brainwashed* by Tom Burrell. In those books are the blueprints for reconditioning the minds of blacks for the purpose of elevation and empowerment. You see, this has been analyzed, thought out and calculated. What some black leaders are speaking of is not simply an illusion or wishful think-ing: there is a movement within the undercurrent of the struggle of blacks in America and abroad. There is a remnant with the knowledge and the passion to infect the masses.

It is also important to understand vertical economics as a vital component of black group economics. Vertical economics is the prac-tice of creating ownership at every level in a specific industry. In other words, ownership at the retail level of the beauty supply industry alone creates a huge weakness, allowing those who possess ownership in distribution and manufacturing to effectively price out black retail businesses; however black ownership at every level—vertical economics—solidifies black control of the industry at every level.

It is economic empowerment that underwrites the vote of blacks as well as their protests. We only need to look at the recent events that have unfolded over the last six months. The killing of young black men by white police officers is alarming. According to a CNN report, young black men are 21 times more likely to be shot and killed by police than are their white counterparts.[2] This only provides a minimal amount of illumination into just how significant this problem actually is. According to the current numbers, young black men are killed by white police officers at a rate of two per week. If consideration is given to other white people in positions of authority, such as security guards and neighborhood watchmen, this number increases to one every 28 hours. It is these types of killings that have sparked mass protests across America; however, blacks have experienced very little in the way of justice and reform, further exacerbating the matter.

It is important for blacks to understand that our lack of political influence is directly associated with our economic impotence. Without the financial power to back and underwrite our protests, they simply become a collective temper tantrum—having no power to bring about change.

With this being said, it is important to understand our history from an economic perspective. At the end of chattel slavery in Amer-

---

[2] Eric Bradner, "Factcheck: Grim Statistics on Race and Police Killings," *CNN*, http://www.cnn.com/2014/12/02/politics/kristoff-oreilly-police-shooting-numbers-fact-check/index.html (accessed June 24, 2015).

ica, the 300,000 quasi-free blacks in this country owned one-half of one percent of this nation's wealth. Here we are 150 years removed from chattel slavery, and yet we still own only one-half of one percent of this nation's aggregate wealth. This is not by accident; it is by design. There is no way for a group of people to compete in a capitalist (free enterprise) economic system without wealth in the form of ownership and control of financial assets such as real estate, stocks and a cash reserve. We have increased our earning potential, but we have failed to properly invest for the purpose of developing wealth.

According to Dr. Claud Anderson, one of the brightest minds in the black community, the fact that blacks never received their 40 acres and a mule is highly indicative of the causation of the perpetual state of oppression of blacks in America.[3] Dr. Anderson is, by far, the greatest champion of African American economic empowerment. He says, "Blacks are trapped in the lowest level of a real life monopoly game." Take a quick look at what else Dr. Anderson has to say about the current economic situation of blacks, and the historical context that gives meaning to our current situation:

> Blacks are America's only non-immigrant group and one of the oldest populations. They have been here since the 1500s and were here before 98 percent of all immigrant groups arrived. Yet blacks are on the bottom of every economic, social, health, and political indicator.[4]

It is important to understand that the economic disenfranchisement of blacks is not a coincidental occurrence. It is not the result of the lack of effort from a group of people who are inherently lazy.

---

[3] Dr. Claud Anderson, *Black Labor, White Wealth: The Search for Power and Economic Justice* (Edgewood, MD: Duncan & Duncan, 1994).

[4] Ibid.

When I hear that argument, it really ignites my rage. How can anyone ever refer to blacks as being lazy, when it was blacks who labored for centuries to build the wealth that this nation now enjoys? How can a group of people who descend from slaves who worked so hard that it was not uncommon for them to have their muscles detach from the bone be lazy?[5] The economic disenfranchisement of blacks in America is the product of a systematic process that is designed to keep blacks poor, ignorant and divided.

There is no way that any group of people can compete without economic fluidity and power. The focus that white supremacy has invested in keeping blacks broke and ignorant has been well placed. Not only are blacks powerless in this position, but they lack the knowledge of how to develop power.

It is this state of economic impotence conjoined with other psychological factors that present the greatest challenge to authentic black empowerment. As we move through this book, you will be introduced to concepts that reveal how economic impotence supports the mis-education of black youth in America.

THE LACK OF CULTURAL INFLUENCE

Because blacks have no economic power, we also lack the capacity to positively impact our culture. Whether you examine the TV shows that pervade our culture or the music that is in constant rotation, you will find negative messages that are being subliminally inculcated into the black psyche. According to Tom Burrell, author of *Brainwashed: Challenging the Myth of Black Inferiority*, it is the propaganda mechanism of mass media that has consistently perpetuated the negative

[5] Joy DeGruy, *Post Traumatic Slave Syndrome: America's Legacy of Enduring Injury and Healing* (Portland, OR: Joy DeGruy Publications, 2005).

image of black inferiority and other negative stereotypes associated with being black. Look at what Burrell has to say about propaganda and its influence on black culture:

> Propaganda is the outer layer of this brainwashing onion. In the marketing world, propaganda is the first tool of persuasion. Brainwashing is the outcome, but propaganda got us here, and its continued use keeps the inferior/superior mind game in play. Instead of using torture and other coercive techniques, the stealthy, media-savvy propagandist uses mass media and other forms of communication to change minds and mold ways of thinking. I have no intention of shying away from the term propaganda. I say we use it—take what was thrown at us, shuck it off, and replace it with "positive" propaganda.[6]

As long as we have no economic power, we will lack the power to influence the black collective, leaving us in a vulnerable state in which we will be influenced by the mass messaging machine of white supremacy. The educational systems that are currently in place are simply mechanisms that are used to reinforce the existing paradigms of inferiority. It is our responsibility to effectively and comprehensively educate our own youth. It is important that we understand the importance of expanding the educational process beyond the acquisition of academic skills. We must equip our youth with a new mindset that understands the importance of building wealth through the practice of black group economics.

We must make a commitment to creating our own systems of mass communication, so that we can create and disseminate mass messages with a positive focus directed at our people. It is our responsi-

---

[6] Tom Burrell, *Brainwashed: Challenging the Myth of Black Inferiority* (New York: Smiley Books, 2010).

bility to teach our youth about our rich heritage. Currently, the vast majority of blacks believe slavery is the totality of African American history. That very concept is damaging because the only image of self is that of subjugation and inferiority. The truth is that slavery should be taught in its proper context, as an interruption to African history, not the totality of it, opening the black mind to the possibility of reclaiming our inherent greatness.

SELF-HATRED

This is a sore subject among blacks, but its forces run deep into the African American psyche. The consistent barrage of messages that create the image of black inferiority, inherently creates the desire of blacks to achieve a certain level of superiority by assimilating to the image of white superiority. This means that blacks have historically sought to change their appearance and position to place themselves in closer relation to their white counterparts—believing that this would somehow improve their status. This means that they have bought into the lie that they are inferior. This can be seen in the fact that a significant amount of blacks view naturally curly or kinky hair as being "bad" hair, while straight hair, which is generally perceived as a European feature, is considered good air. The comparisons are multitudinous, but the end result is the same—self-hatred.

A great deal of money is spent by blacks in the attempt to change their appearance to look more European. This is highly indicative of the psychological makeup of blacks in America. The self-image is something that is shaped at a very early age, and it is in these formative years that the black subconscious is riddled with a consistent message of inferiority. It was these types of messages that were necessary to create a more docile and subjugated slave.

This means that we must take the time to rebuild pride in the black self-conscious. This is best done in the early years of a person's life. This is why the educational process through which our kids are informed of "self" is immensely important. We cannot expect white America to properly educate our children; that is our responsibility. We must introduce our children to their true heritage and history, so that they can develop a healthy self-esteem and self-image, eliminating the devastating force of self-hatred.

THE DISINTEGRATION OF THE BLACK FAMILY NUCLEUS

This topic definitely deserves its own volume, and I plan to dedicate myself to producing one in the near future; however, it is worth, at least, placing the cards on the table here. The all but complete decimation of the black family has caused widespread devastation that can be seen in every sphere of the black existence.

I have stated this on more than one occasion, and I will endeavor to present it once more. As a race of people, blacks will only ascend as high as our women can spiritually elevate us, and we will only go as far as our men can physically lead us; yet it must be understood that this conquest for advancement requires the presence and participation of both the black man and the black woman.

Here is the problem, we were designed to function as a nuclear unit. It is through the family that information is initially disseminated and core beliefs are formed. It is the family that is the nucleus of civilization—one of the four prominent institutions in any form of civil and social culture.

Since we arrived on this continent more than 400 years ago, there has been an all-out assault against the black family. Because slaves were considered property, they had no legal right to marry, and even the makeshift weddings that they participated in had no power to protect them from being split up and sold away from one another by their masters. In fact, slaves were systematically bred and separated to keep them from formulating family bonds that would inherently provide them with internal strength and direction.

The psychological scars that were suffered during slavery followed the black man and the black woman into their physical freedom—ensuring that they remained bound psychologically—and just when blacks began to develop some sense of filial responsibility and commitment, white supremacy racism introduced the feminist movement into the black community. This served to further exacerbate existing issues while creating new ones.

The infiltration of thought processes that convinced the black woman that she was being oppressed and held back by the black man, led to her despising her traditional role as a domestic caregiver and educator of the children. She saw corporate America and the American job market as the source of her liberation. It was her chance to break away from her man.

What the black woman did not consider was how her exodus from the black home to invade the workforce would impact her family, especially the children. With no mother in the home, the primary caregiving responsibility transferred to the daycare and public education systems. It entrusted a system with educating our young black youth in which the majority of teachers were middle-aged white women. We gave the responsibility of empowering our children to people who had no interest whatsoever in doing so.

The social programs of the late 1960s also served to create separation and distance between the black man and the black woman. While white farmers were able to benefit from American subsidies and still preserve a family unit, blacks were offered certain financial subsidies including housing; however, these subsidies came with a covert stipulation that disallowed the presence of a man in the home. So at a time when the black man was struggling to find consistent employment, his woman was being enticed with government support, and all she had to do was become the head of the household—thus alienating the father figure.

To exacerbate this destructive mechanism, the current child support system was implemented as a failsafe. Not only is the child support system heavily weighted against the black male, but it is often used as leverage by black women to settle personal scores with their ex. The system also provides another conduit through which the Private Prison Industrial Complex is fed a steady dose of black inmates.

While the black woman has played her role in the demise of the black family nucleus, the black man is not without fault. Far too many black men have become consumed with self-gratifying quests. They have chosen to abdicate their roles as leaders, protectors and providers. They have chosen to procreate[7] and then abandon their progeny.[8] The black man has become completely self-consumed.

The lack of upward mobility in the black community is inextricably bound to multi-generational poverty and the destruction of the black nuclear family. Again, one of the best ways to address this issue is early in the developmental stages of a black child's life. By reinforcing the importance of the family structure, and teaching little girls how to respect little boys and teaching little boys how to care for and protect little girls.

---

[7] Procreate: breed, produce, reproduce, multiply.

[8] Progeny: seed, offspring.

RELIGION AS AN EDUCATIONAL MECHANISM

Religion has been one of the most effective tools used by white supremacy to assist in the process of subjugation.[9] Actually, the use of religion to condition and control the minds of a conquered people is nothing new. Throughout history, conquering nations have used their cultural religion as a method of brainwashing and conditioning those whom they have conquered.

When it comes to Christianity, the primary mode of religious conditioning in America, especially when it comes to Americans of African descent, it is somewhat ironic. This is due to the fact that one of the primary themes of the Bible—the authoritative source of Christianity—is the conquering and subjugation of the Israelites as a form of punishment for turning away from God. One specific area in which this is presented in lucid fashion, is in the book of Daniel.

To provide a brief synopsis of the story, over the course of three separate invasions of Jerusalem, King Nebuchadnezzar and his Chaldean military besieged Jerusalem—the first time was in 605 B.C. During the first invasion, Nebuchadnezzar allowed Jehoiakim to remain on the throne as a vassal king. It was at this time that Daniel, Hananiah, Mishael and Azariah (with the last three being more commonly known by their slave names—Shadrach, Meshach and Abednego) were taken captive and taken back to Babylon. This entire book is replete with stories in which either Daniel or the other three Hebrew boys had to resist the religious tenets of the Chaldean culture. I know that there are some of you who are wondering who are the Chaldeans. Most people view them as Babylonians; however, the new empire established by Nabopolassar—the father of Nebuchad-

---

[9] Subjugation: defeat, suppression, conquest, oppress.

nezzar—also created the Chaldean empire when he conquered the Assyrians in Babylon.

In Chapter one of the story, the king orders that the young boys be fed the delicacies of the royal family; nevertheless, the boys realized that this was a part of the brainwashing process, and they subsequently convinced their overseer to allow them to have a vegetarian diet. The next time there was an issue was in Chapter three, when everyone was ordered to bow and worship the new image that Nebuchadnezzar had built. Shadrach, Meshach, and Abednego refused and were sentenced to be cast into the fiery furnace—which they survived. I am not here to defend the story, only to point out the psychological implications. Later in the book, Daniel would insist on praying during a time when prayer was banned, and he would be cast into a den of lions—a fate he also survived.

What is to be understood here is the fact that by resisting to conform to the religious tenets of their captors, these young boys were able to maintain their sense of identity. When a conquered people assume the religion of their conquerors, they will become confused as to their own identity and self-worth. Religions are built around the cultures of the people who create them, and they are not meant to support the alien psyche of a conquered people. What cannot go unnoticed in all of this is that at the same time that the conqueror is forcing his religion upon those that have been conquered, he is also outlawing the practice of their native religion.

Understanding the psychology behind this provides the foundation for gaining a lucid apprehension of how white supremacy has used Christianity as one of its most powerful weapons against African Americans. Not only does the relinquishment of our native religion come at the price of surrendering a substantial amount of our spiritual assets in exchange for an emotional experience, but it also introduces an inferiority complex. It is impossible for a group of people to maintain a positive and healthy self-image when the religion that they are practicing presents a God that does not look like them, but is identical to their captors.

Although the largest portion of this book is centered on the American educational system, it is paramount for Blacks to understand that there are many methodologies being used to mis-educate our people, and we must successfully engage each one of them.

Even if

NEGROES

do successfully imitate the whites,
nothing new has thereby been
accomplished. You simply have a
larger number of persons doing
what others have been doing.
The unusual gifts of the race
have not thereby been developed,
and an unwilling world, therefore
continues to wonder that the
Negro is good for.

Carter G. Woodson
The Mis-education of the Negro
1933

Chapter 2
An Identity Crisis

One of the most devastating impacts of slavery is that it robbed
blacks of their true identity. The knowledge of self is paramount to
the advancement of any people, and blacks are no different. The psychological legacy of slavery is a poor self-image that is fostered by
the lack of the knowledge of self. This was accomplished through a
complex system of subjugation in which an entire group of people
was forcefully removed from their own land and taken to a foreign
country where they were stripped of their religion, their history and
their name.

Slaves were given the last names of their slave masters to represent
the fact that they were property and that they had no rights. This was
also a very subtle method of blurring the lines of identity. In a culture
such as the one in America, very little emphasis is placed on the chosen or surname of an individual. But a person's name has an immense
impact on their sense of identity and their self-image. In many eastern
cultures—including many African cultures—a great deal goes into
choosing the name of a newborn. The name will have a direct impact
on the child's self-image.

In many of these eastern cultures, names are often extracted from
the family tree or related to specific events that took place during the
pregnancy.[1] In whatever process that was used to choose the name, it

[1] H. Edward Deluzain, *Names and Personality*, Behind the Name, 1996.

had meaning and it established the baseline of what that child was to expect from themselves. To take away a name from a slave and then to give them a new name that was indicative of their current situation allowed slave masters to lay the foundation for optimal subjugation.

It was not only the renaming of slaves through which this dynamic took its toll. The fact that the right and authority for a slave to choose the name for their progeny was not completely theirs also contributed to the identity crisis. The manipulation of names for the sake of control is nothing new, it has been done for centuries. It was a common practice for a conquering nation to change the names of those conquered as a method of stripping away their identity.

It was Sigmund Freud that brought further illumination to the importance of a name to a person's identity. Freud noticed that the association between a person and their name can be seen at the most rudimentary levels of communication, such as answering a phone or introducing another or one's self. When answering a phone or introducing one's self, a person always says, "Hello, this is…" or Hi, I am…" Rarely do we see or hear people introduce themselves by saying, "Hi, my name is…" The phrases "I am" and "this is" are identifying clauses.

Because humans identify with our names, our names impact how we view ourselves. It is a connection to our past and a direct link to our ancestors. When that link is abruptly broken, it has an immense impact on our sense and knowledge of self.

SEPARATION FROM OUR HISTORY

Unfortunately, losing the sense of self that is associated with one's name was not the only factor that slaves had to grapple with in the battle to maintain their identity. Slaves were completely severed from their history. It was considered a crime, punishable by death, to discuss their history among themselves. Their white masters understood that their history was rich and powerful, and allowing slaves to develop a direct correlation with their history would prove counterproductive: robbing the slaves of their history was another link in the chain of psychological bondage and oppression. The white supremacy system understood that physical bondage could only be perpetuated over the long-term when the minds of the oppressed were more bound by the limitations of poor self-esteem and an inferiority complex.

It is important to realize that each of the issues that are being unfolded in this book have a dynamic that is so complex that it needs to be examined in great detail in its own context. Chapters upon chapters can be written on the devastating impact of ripping away the history of a people. One of the most devastating and lasting effects of this phenomenon is the existing lack of affinity that blacks feel toward our own history as well as the lack of passion invested in learning about our history.

After several generations of disallowing black slaves to partici-pate in native religions or to discuss their history, the "knowledge of self" began to slip away, until there was little left in the minds of slaves to share with their progeny. To exacerbate the matter, the gap in the knowledge of their history left slaves immensely vulnerable to the interpolation of erroneous historical and religious concepts by whites. Black history was replaced with the European version of history, which favored those of European descent and placed blacks in a negative and subservient light.

In addition to the distortion of history, white slave masters also forced the whitewashed version of Christianity upon slaves. Although slaves were initially only allowed to attend church with their masters, eventually, slave owners would select and ordain black slaves as ministers. This vassal form of leadership actually proved to be one of the most pernicious[2] mechanisms and vices of control during slavery. The ministers who were chosen had displayed a high sense of loyalty to their masters, and they lacked the inherent traits of a natural leader, meaning that they posed no threat to their masters. They were given specific instructions on what they were to teach, and how it was to be taught. They received explicit instructions on how slavery was to be addressed from a biblical perspective. When slavery was mentioned by a black ordained preacher, the slave was always black and the master was always white.

Additionally, another immeasurable force that was used to disengage slaves from any true sense of identity was the powerful force of imagery. Not only was Christianity forced upon them, but the image of a white Jesus—an image that was representative of their oppressor—was also an incessant force that they had to deal with. When you cannot relate to the God that you serve, it leads to an identity crisis. When the God you serve resembles your oppressor, it sends a message that your oppressors are innately superior. It also sends a message that your oppressed state is your lot in life—you were designed to be a servant.

THE MANIFESTATION OF THE IDENTITY CRISIS

There are multitudinous ways that the identity crisis has manifested itself in the current black culture, such as self-hatred and the exaltation of everything white. It is a natural human proclivity to aspire to those things that are viewed as excellent and great. The lack of a lucid and veracious[3] identity, led many blacks to aspire to some

[2] Pernicious: highly injurious or destructive: deadly.

[3] Veracious: Honest and straight forward

form of being white. This caused black men and women to seek to straighten their hair, because straight hair was associated with being European. Many were inspired to mix races for the purpose of producing offspring with a lighter complexion.

Without a knowledge of self, a person will search for something to identify with. They will look to those things and people that they consider to be greater than themselves. A great deal of effort has been expended to present the image of white superiority, while simultaneously suggesting the inferiority of blacks. Because blacks do not collectively have a sense of identity, they are subject to the suggestions of white supremacy that they assimilate into its system. This is why you see so many blacks that will suggest that the struggles that most blacks experience—whether it is police harassment or discrimination in the workplace—is because blacks fail to assimilate.

HOW DOES THE EDUCATION SYSTEM FACTOR IN?

You can actually look at the entire black experience in America as being one long 400-year experiment in mis-education. Blacks have been fed a consistent dose of false propaganda, in multitudinous forms, for the purpose of subjugating us and creating a permanent working class that will ensure that the rich elite maintain their positions of power. The education system is only one lever in this massive machine of mis-education; nevertheless, it must be given a great deal of weight because it is the mechanism that serves to reinforce the negative image of blacks, distort the history of blacks and condition blacks for a role of subservience—even at the highest levels.

Our schools don't prepare our children to be independent thinkers. Our schools are not designed to introduce young black children to the idea of entrepreneurship. The current school system in America serves three primary purposes:

1. To prepare those who are able to successfully navigate the maleficent snares and obstacles set out for black children for a life in corporate America, where they will work diligently to enrich the wealthy.

2. To condition the minds of young black girls who find themselves struggling within the system for a life of poverty and dependence on the government for support.

3. To prepare our young black boys for their travel through the school to prison pipeline where they will help to enrich those who have invested in the Private Prison Industrial Complex.

Year after year, we send our children to schools that purposely withhold and distort history to the benefit of Europeans. This only serves to reinforce the negative propaganda that our children are inculcating into their psyche through their exposure to other mediums such as TV and radio.

It is important that I digress for a moment here. With all of the evidence that will be presented in this book to reveal the malicious machinations of white supremacy and its methodologies for miseducating our youth, it is imperative that you understand that it is our responsibility to ensure that our children are properly educated, and that is one of the primary themes of this book. It is not simply to show that our children are not being properly educated, but it is to highlight the fact that we are failing them when we allow this to take place.

The education system emphatically contributes to the nebulosity associated with the black identity crisis. Education is the one tool that has the power to shift the paradigms through which African Americans see themselves.

When there is no sense of self, blacks will assimilate into the racist system by default. Dr. Umar Johnson has been quoted as saying, "White supremacy is absolutely nothing without black conformance."[4] What he is saying is that the existence of white supremacy isn't the problem for blacks in America or abroad, but the problem is that we acquiesce to the system as we attempt to conform. Conformity is a necessity in the empowerment of any system.

Conformity to an oppressive system does not serve to alleviate its pressure. Conversely, it serves to further weaken the oppressed. As long as blacks are fighting to fit in, we will continue to be at the mercy of those whose acceptance and approbation we seek. Before we can ever truly experience empowerment and elevation, we must become intimately acquainted with self—not who our former captors and current oppressors have told us we are—but the true self that is inextricably bound to our ancient heritage and history.

Until we develop an affinity with the greatness of our past, we will never be adequately equipped to experience greatness in the future. The knowledge of self is apropos to the achievement of greatness as a collective. Organizations, such as the Nation of Islam, have long used the knowledge of self to institute reforms in the thought processes of black men and women. This has proven successful because it is a part of the natural development of the black psyche. It is the same system that Ancient African teachers used more than 4,000 years ago in the Nile Valley.[5]

Europeans have done an exceptional job of ensuring that their version of history has been effectively passed along to their progeny,

[4] Dr. Umar Johnson, "Black Compliance is Not the Answer to White Supremacy," *The Odyssey Consortium 2014*, www.theodysseyproject21.com/category/editorials/page/4/. (accessed June 23, 2015).

[5] Dr. Na'im Akbar, *Breaking the Chains of Psychological Slavery* (Tallahassee, FL: Mind Productions Publications, 1996).

consequently keeping their identity intact. We must become committed to bringing an even higher level of veracity to the stating of our history and legacy.

EDUCATED INTO DUMBNESS!

As I survey the economic and political landscape of this nation and how it inevitably impacts blacks in this country, I am forced to come to grips with the fact that although we are becoming more educated in some realms, we are actually slipping into a deep intellectual and spiritually comatose state, in which we will become even more vulnerable to the evil machinations of our oppressors.

THE FALLACIOUS ADAGE

There is an old adage that is often quoted within the confines of many classrooms and college auditoriums. How many times have you heard, "There is no stupid question?" The truth is that there are stupid questions. No, it is not the question that seems irrational or misplaced that I would readily and emphatically deem to be stupid. The question that I speak of here is that question that is raised without critical thought having been applied to the dilemma. When the question is asked before ever taking the time to work through the labyrinthine corridors of the natural process of reason, then the question is not only stupid, but it is a form of intellectual lethargy.

We have been conditioned to ask before we think. We seek to have others answer our questions before we have endeavored to answer them ourselves. Why is this stupid? It demands very little of ourselves and it places too much trust in the hands of someone, who does not have a true vested interest in what we will become based on the information provided, or that vested interest is best served by disseminating erroneous information or concepts into the psyche of those being affected by that information.

HOW WE HAVE BEEN EDUCATED INTO DUMBNESS

The concept of being educated into dumbness is actually a paradigm that has been extracted from one of the core philosophies of the late Dr. Amos Wilson. Dr. Wilson passionately made the point that the cultural differences and historical polarities between Europeans and Blacks dictate that they cannot equally benefit from the same educational curriculum. What this means is that a black student that is exposed to the exact same program as a white student, who is equally successful in completing the course will not benefit from the course in the same manner as the white student.

There are many influences that explain this phenomenon; however, the void created by the absence of critical thought leaves the black student at a disadvantage because the intellectual stimuli that he or she receives is not representative of their culture, background or general reality. Without critical thought and exposure to those things that are culturally relative, we will continue to be consumed by a system that is designed to perpetuate our demise.

CRITICAL THOUGHT PRODUCES EXPONENTIAL POWER

As we press inexorably[6] toward greater heights as a people, we must break away from the natural proclivity to have others answer questions that we ourselves have the power and intellect to answer on our own. There must be a high level of digression from business as usual. We must become engrossed in our own affairs and the seeking of our own solutions. Critical thought drives creativity. Critical

[6] Inexorably: relentlessly, adamantly, obdurately.

27

thought will generate the momentum necessary to create the paradigmatic shifts that are paramount to us rising as a people. Yes, there are stupid questions when you are the living answer. We must free our children to engage critical thought as a part of their holistic educational process.

TRUE BLACK CONSCIOUSNESS!

Toward the end of the 19th century and the early part of the 20th century, there were a number of brilliant minds, such as Marcus Garvey, Carter G. Woodson, Martin Delaney, George G.M. James, W.E.B. DuBois, J.A. Rogers, among others, who lit and carried the torch of restoration for the black identity. This paved the way for those who would later follow.

In the middle of the 20th century, there was another surge of exceptional black minds that served to reignite the torch of restoration for the black identity. Great minds, such as Chancellor Williams, Dr. John Henrik Clarke, Dr. Yosef Ben Jochannon, John G. Jackson, Asa Hilliard, Dr. Frances Cress-Welsing, Molefi Asante and others presented a new image of the African American that was diametrically[7] opposed to the one that was being presented by the white mainstream media.

The gulf that separated the enlightened was bridged by the brilliant mind of Dr. Claud Anderson, who opened the door for great minds such as Dr. Na'im Akbar, Dr. Joy DeGruy, and the late Dr. Amos Wilson and many of their contemporaries.

These great minds have paved the way for the ultimate black consciousness experience; but we must learn to get out of our own way. The black consciousness movement is not about self-celebration and

---

[7] Diametrically: wholly, completely, absolutely.

self-aggrandizement. It is not about self-promotion for the purpose of increased status or earning the approbation of the masses. The ultimate responsibility of those who have become enlightened is to infuse their knowledge into the collective for the purpose of empowering the masses. This can have no greater impact than when it is given to our youth in their most impressionable years.

It is immensely important that our youth develop a healthy self-image that is directly associated with the totality of who they are. The history books in the class room only tell the story of slavery, and the story is rendered from a slanted scale that lacks veracity and depth. This abridged story of our history offers glimpses into our past, and it briefly explains how we arrived at where we are today. Yet it lacks the depth and distance to provide the complete portrait of who we are.

It is vital that we make the connection between where we stand today and where we started. We must show our youth that there are no limitations beyond what their minds can conceive. We have seen what the belief of no limitations on the basketball court could produce. Young black men like Magic Johnson and Michael Jordan revolutionized the sport. But we are so much more than a physically gifted people. What will happen when our children are made aware of the fact that there are no limitations in the worlds of academia, science, business or the science of the human mind? How much further will they aspire to go? How much greater will they become?

We must provide our children with something to celebrate. Self-celebration is a part of the natural process of growth; still, most of our children have been given very little to celebrate about themselves. They need to know that they descend from greatness and royalty, and that their ancestors made massive contributions to civilization and technology. Tariq Nasheed and his Hidden Colors series has done wonders to bring enlightenment to the black collective; however, there has to be more done in this manner.

We also need to learn how to celebrate ourselves, because celebration is a part of the healing process. We must demand, through our actions that we be allowed to tell our story in our way. We can no longer be willing to allow others to tell their version of our story. It is time that we celebrate our heritage, our greatness and our potential.

I challenge each of you to look beyond yourself and see your purpose, that thing which is greater than you. Allow your purpose to ignite a genuine passion within you to empower our people. That is when we will begin to see change. Individualism is one of the most destructive forces present in the black community. Let unity be our battle cry, and our children become our unrelenting passion.

If they took the idea that they could
escape poverty through education,
I think it would make a more basic
and long-lasting change in the way
things happen. What we need are
positive, realistic goals and the
willingness to work. Hard work and
practical goals.

Kareem Abdul-Jabbar

1990

Chapter 3

The Psycho-Academic War Against Black Boys

As with the majority of chapters is this book, this topic deserves attention and needs much more consideration than I am able to give it in this one volume. Nevertheless, I will endeavor to shed substantial light on the matter. I would suggest reading *Psycho-Academic Holocaust: The Special Education & ADHD War Against Black Boys* by Dr. Umar Johnson. My goal for this chapter is to highlight the malignant and devastating mechanisms that are directed specifically at black males, beginning as early as five years old.

Be forewarned that some of the information that will be presented in this chapter will be highly contested and highly controversial. Nevertheless, I believe it is all an integral part of the entire portrait that needs to be painted for blacks in America. The attack on our young boys is a significant piece of a much larger puzzle which involves a focused assault on the image and masculinity of black men. Although it runs much deeper than this, at the core, the assault against black men is the result of an inherent fear of black men by whites, especially white men.

In order to gain a significant apprehension of the war on black boys, it is important to understand the relevance of marginalizing the black male and the black male image. White supremacy understands that the way to subdue a group of people is through their leadership. The emasculation of the black male has been a goal of the white supremacy machine since the first slaves arrived on American soil, and great effort has been exerted over the course of the last 400 years to keep the black man from collectively resuming his natural role as a leader, provider and protector of his family and community. I will open this up in greater detail in chapter 10.

Steps have been taken to confuse the role of black men, to promote effeminate traits, and over the last 40 years, there has been a persistent effort to homosexualize the black male. The subtle strategies that have been employed have, in many ways, been highly effective; yet the stealthy strategies that have been implemented have been so subtle that many deny their existence. The problem is that the end result is undeniable. What many have simply attributed to a natural process of degradation of the social culture has actually been a well-designed strategy designed to minimize the effectiveness of the male role.

When you understand that the black race will only be able to go as far as our black men can lead us, you will begin to understand why it is so important to minimize the impact and effectiveness of the black man to lead. The strong, masculine black man poses a significant threat to the current order, and white supremacy is committed to neutralizing this threat.

THE INTRODUCTION OF EUGENICS

I really wish that I had more time to contribute to this one topic, but I do not want to detract too much from the overall theme of mis-education. Nevertheless, it is imperative to present a brief history of eugenics and how it plays a role in the mis-education of our youth. In its generic form, eugenics is a word that is derived from the Greek word *eugenes*, meaning "well-born." This places emphasis on the production of progeny from a superior gene pool; therefore, eugenics is the belief and practice of taking measures to improve the current genetic quality of the human population—on local, national and global levels. As part of the process of practicing eugenics, Margaret Sanger, being financially backed by William Gates, the father of Microsoft founder Bill Gates, launched what was then known as the Negro Project. The eugenicist theory was a prevailing ideology in the early 20th century, and Margaret Sanger took significant steps to align herself with eugenicists who espoused racial purity and supremacy.[1]

It was the primary goal of eugenicists to purify the Aryan race through encouraging the fit to reproduce with the fit and the unfit to restrict reproduction altogether. Margaret Sanger followed the tenets of Malthusian Eugenics, a eugenics philosophy founded by Thomas Robert Malthus, a 19th century professor of political economy. Malthus believed an existing population time bomb presented a threat to the human race. He considered certain social issues, such as deprivation, poverty and hunger as empirical evidence of the population crisis.

Below is a quote from an essay written and published by Malthus in 1798:

> All children born, beyond what would be required to keep up the population to a desired level, must necessarily perish, unless room is made for them by the deaths of grown persons. We should facilitate, instead of foolishly and vainly endeavoring to impede, the operations of nature producing this mortality.[2]

---

[1] Tanya L. Green, "The Negro Project: Margaret Sanger's Eugenic Plan for Black America, Black Genocide," *Concerned Women for America*, http://www.cwfa.org/the-negro-project-margaret-sangers-eugenic-plan-for-black-americans/ (accessed June 23, 2015).

[2] Thomas Robert Malthus, *Principle of Population* (London: John Murray, 1798).

Sanger, like many other whites, had a very low opinion of blacks and their genetic makeup, and so she devised a plan to significantly reduce the population through the abortion of unborn black children and the sterilization of black women. This was known as the Negro Project. In 1917, Sanger founded *The Birth Control Review*, a publication that she used to propagate her pro-eugenic ideas. Sanger's organization, the American Birth Control League, which would eventually become Planned Parenthood, continued to use the publication as a platform to support eugenic ideas, even after Sanger stopped being editor in 1929.

In one article, Sanger wrote:

> It [charity] encourages the healthier and more normal sections of the world to shoulder the burden of unthinking and indiscriminate fecundity of others; which brings with it, as I think the reader will agree, a dead weight of human waste. Instead of decreasing and aiming to eliminate the stocks that are most detrimental to the future of the race and the world, it tends to render them, to a menacing degree, dominant.

She concluded,

> The most serious charge that can be brought against modern 'benevolence' is that it encourages the perpetuation of defectives, delinquents, and dependents. These are the most dangerous elements in the world community, the most devastating curse on human progress and expression.

It was in 1939 that Sanger created the Negro Project, a eugenics-based program that was focused on reducing the black population. She even recruited black ministers to help make the black community more accepting of the ideology associated with her actions:

We should hire three or four colored ministers, preferably with social service backgrounds, and with engaging personalities. The most successful educational approach to the Negro is through religious appeal. We don't want the word to go out that we want to exterminate the Negro population, and the minister is the man who can straighten out that idea if it ever occurs in any of their more rebellious members.[3]

In another of many excerpts quoting Sanger, she asserts that those with unfit genes should be given the choice of sterilization or segregation: "Give dysgenic groups [those with bad genes] in our population their choice of segregation or sterilization."

Today, abortion remains one of the most powerful levers of population control. It is estimated that since 1973, more than 14 million black children have been aborted. Statistics reveal that black fetuses are being aborted at a rate of 1,800 per day.

You may be asking what does this have to do with the mis-education of black youth. This train of thought points to the idea of population control, which actually plays out as an element in the mis-education of black youth. More directly, it places miseducated black girls in the crosshairs of a system that aims at reducing the black population through abortion, and the perpetuation of black poverty through government-funded social programs.

THE EFFEMINIZATION AND HOMOSEXUALIZATION OF THE BLACK MALE IMAGE

As far as young black men are concerned, it helps us to understand the mindset behind a number of nefarious schemes designed to reduce and exploit the black population. In 1952, John D. Rockefeller

---

[3] Margaret Sanger, *Woman, Morality, and Birth Control* (New York: American Birth Control League, 1922), 12.

founded the World Population Council. This organization functions like a think tank to develop strategies to control and manipulate the population on a global level. It was the idea of this think tank to use homosexuality as a form of population control. Up until 1973, homosexuality was listed in the *Diagnostic and Statistical Manual of Mental Disorders* as a form of psychosis or mental disorder; however, in 1973 a stealth campaign was waged to convince psychiatrists to vote to have it removed from the manual. In 1974, a campaign was launched by Henry Kissinger to consider homosexuality as a viable form of population control in the black community.

From Kissinger's campaign to use homosexuality as a mechanism of population control, an organized machination[4] was devised to integrate homosexuality into the black community on a mass scale. At the same time a campaign was launched to create a new image of homosexuality—one that is more acceptable and even applauded. This approach to make homosexuality more appealing served two ends. It pleased the gay agenda, which was growing in its power at an exponential rate. Additionally, it gave Kissinger and all who were looking for a way to reduce the black population what they wanted—more feminized black men.

This is an extremely important fact when discussing the mis-education of black youth, because one of the primary goals associated with the mis-education of black boys, specifically, is to effeminize or homosexualize the black male image. Now, this accomplishes much more than population control. It helps to ease the natural fear of black men by white men. It also slowly introduces a new paradigm of homosexual supremacy that is being systematically inculcated into the black psyche through the public education system.

[4] Machination: Scheme, plot or plan.

The public education system has three primary goals of mis-education:

- To foster self-hatred and a black inferiority complex
- To establish white love and a white superiority complex
- To effeminize and/or homosexualize the black male image

The system is designed to marginalize young black boys in multitudinous ways. A great deal is made of the exorbitant dropout rate among black boys, but Dr. Umar Johnson, who works as an educational psychologist (he diagnoses behavioral and learning disabilities in school-aged children) says that it should be viewed as a push-out rate more than a dropout rate. He further iterates that public schools are designed to alienate and disenfranchise our black boys. In other words, they are not designed to engage the specific issues and needs of young black boys.

In examining this dynamic I have determined that the goal to homosexualize the black male image is considerably more pernicious than most people realize. What most see as a moral or religious issue is more of social and economic issue that consistently places a strain on the black collective in the form of the lack of black male leadership. You see, no matter how successful the gay male may be, he will never be recognized as a leader in the black community, because there is an innate proclivity to look to masculinity for leadership.

Also, the gay man's view of the American Social Order will be different from the average black man, because they have found a sense of acceptance and benevolence in the gay community. It is not in the gay black man's best interest to buck the status quo. In essence, the gay black man knows his place in the current social order and he is actually comfortable with it, meaning there is no real passion to disrupt it.

AN ALIEN WORLD

Statistics reveal that 83 percent of the elementary teaching force is made up of white females. This presents a double-negative experience for young black boys. First of all, black boys have a unique set of issues that can only be effectively engaged by adult black men. At least with a black female teacher, there may be a certain level of genuine empathy concerning the struggles that young black boys face, but a white female cannot effectively empathize with something she cannot understand or relate to.

Honestly, one of the most prevalent problems that black boys face in the inner city is growing up in a single parent household where the parent is predominantly the mother. Without male energy and guidance consistently in the home, the young male child will find himself battling the development of certain traits that are associated with femininity. In addition to this, the young black male is faced with the situation in which he is under the authority of a female, which is innately unnatural to him. If not careful, a single black mother can break the spirit of her son, and she can also create role confusion, negatively impacting the capacity of her son to effectively execute his role as a black man. This is why black single mothers must be very careful in executing dominance over their male children. It creates a reverse role in which the black male is acquiescent to the control and demands of the female.

Now imagine a young black man being placed in a classroom with a white female teacher who has preconceived notions about who he is, how he will behave and what he is capable of achieving. In many cases, his teacher will have a natural fear of him, even at an early age. She will also foster a preconceived notion that he is incapable of learning at the rate of other students. She will have no cultural affinity to the child, limiting her ability to recognize his intellectual genius.

The universalization and standardization of how intellect is measured is highly weighted to appease a Eurocentric frame of reference. In other words, the manner in which intellect is measured in the American public education system is designed to cater to the white culture, and it is hostile toward blacks. Take the IQ test, which is the test that is used to measure intellect in the American school system. It is also the test that is used as a mechanism to disqualify black children from their right to equal access to the same educational environment as whites.

In other words, when the Supreme Court ruled on the *Brown vs Board of Education* case, establishing that color could not be used as a criterion for determining access to schools and educational resources, the educational system had to come up with a way to keep black children away from white kids. The way they did this was through standardized tests that suggests that blacks are intellectually inferior to whites. They used the results of standardized IQ tests to show that black kids consistently tested approximately 15 points lower than white students; however, what they did not reveal is that the test is biased. Here is how.

There are four primary elements of an IQ test, and they are:

- Perceptional Reasoning—which demonstrates the ability to manipulate three-dimensional objects and the ability to solve spatial problems.
- Working memory—includes short term and operational memory, requiring the ability to remember and to effectively process the information that is presented.
- Processing speed—refers to the speed at which an individual

is able to process information and their ability to react to the information.

- Verbal Comprehension—is the ability to encompass reading, writing and communication skills.

Now, what public education officials, and white psychologists will not readily share with the public is the fact that black children do equally well on the first three elements, working memory, processing speed, and perceptional reasoning. In fact, they do better in many cases than other children. Where black children struggle is in the area of verbal comprehension. Actually, there is a simple and reasonable explanation for this. The first three elements are authentic measurements of a child's intellect, meaning that it tests skills that are not learned, but are a natural part of the child's intellect. However, the last element, verbal comprehension, because it uses a specific vernacular, benefits the child who is naturally exposed to that vernacular, while penalizing the child to which this vernacular is foreign. Vocabulary is learned, therefore it is not an effective measurement of intellect.

It is immensely important that the myth of black inferiority continue to be perpetrated. It is a key link in the chain that propels white supremacy. Therefore, certain measuring tools like IQ tests are consistently used to disqualify black students, especially young black males.

A white female teacher, functioning in a white educational system, is about as distant from a young black boy as can possibly be accomplished. She has no true frame of reference. She has no affinity to his life experience. She is not reflective of anything that he can associate with or respect. In fact, her very existence is a source of great frustration as he searches to find himself.

At the first sign of trouble, she will attempt to have him evaluated for some type of learning or behavioral disorder. This will serve to remove him from her class, increasing her level of comfort, while sending him down a perilous path of disenfranchisement and isolation.

Something that has to be considered is the natural proclivity of a man to resist being dominated and controlled by a woman. Unfortunately, this behavior is often diagnosed as oppositional defiant disorder. You see, basically, disorders have been developed to explain natural behaviors of young black boys in a manner that qualifies them for some level of special education designation. This does not only help to qualify them for disenfranchisement and marginalization, but it also brings medical and legal rationalization to the reality that the mental health community and Big Pharma will profit greatly from his disenfranchisement.

THE SPECIAL EDUCATION CONUNDRUM

To gain a more lucid apprehension of what is taking place in the education system, it is important to understand the special education system and how it is used against our black boys. Special education is a direct response to the desegregation of schools. The 1954 *Brown vs the Board of Education* case, which eventually led to the desegregation of schools, was the catalyst for the development of a new policy that would allow schools to continue the practice of segregation, at least at a certain level.

The Supreme Court Ruling had determined that school districts could no longer use race as a determining factor in choosing the classroom makeup of their schools; on the other hand, the introduction of special education provided the mechanism that would allow the continued separation of students based on disability.

Something that began as a segregation mechanism ended up presenting white supremacy with even greater influence in their quest to control the thought processes of blacks in America, and it opened the door for an all-out assault on black boys.

One thing that I would recommend is that every parent get a copy of the *Diagnostic and Statistical Manual of Mental Disorders* (DSM). This is the Bible of psychology and psychiatry, and it lists all of the learning and behavioral disorders that are used to identify children as special needs students requiring special education. The inherent problem is not special education itself, but the overrepresentation of black males in the special education system. According to a special study by Dr. Jamila Codrington, Ph.D. and Dr. Halford H. Fairchild, Ph.D., the overrepresentation of blacks in the special education system has existed for more than four decades.[5] This means that since the special education program was instituted on a national level in 1975, blacks have been specifically targeted at a higher rate than their representation in the general population.

With certain conditions, such as ADHD, learning disability and conduct disorder, mental retardation and oppositional defiant disorder, being used to corral young black boys and herd them off to a form of social ostracization, black boys have been left in a hopeless situation in which they have no representation and no real advocate. Due to the fact that a significant number black parents are simply ignorant to the machinations of white supremacy as implemented through the education system, it is easy to dupe parents into signing consent forms to test their boys for learning disabilities and behavioral disorders that will ultimately qualify them as learning disabled.

---

[5] J. Codrington and H. H. Fairchild, "Special Education and the Mis-education of African American Children: A Call to Action," *Washington, DC: The Association of Black Psychologists 2012*, http://www.abpsi.org/pdf/specialedpositionpaper021312.pdf (accessed June 23, 2015).

We must be willing to stand guard over our boys to protect them from a system that has served to completely derail their development and growth, ultimately steering them toward a life plagued by failure, underachievement and perpetual incarceration.

We must be careful with allowing the system to place these labels on the backs of our children. It sends the message to the child that something is wrong with him. It tells him that he is incapable and he doesn't fit into this system—nurturing his hatred for the education system. What this young boy and his parents are unaware of is that he is being systematically prepared for the school to prison pipeline, which we will discuss in-depth in another chapter.

THE INTRODUCTION OF PSYCHOTROPIC DRUGS

If the psychological devastation associated with this diabolical machination of special education is not enough, the system has introduced the prescribing of psychotropic drugs into the equation. According to the National Institute of Health, there is an expanding problem as far as the use of psychotropic drugs as a means to treat behavioral and learning disorders in special education students. In a recent study, it was revealed that 40 percent of the students being studied were on a medication at their baseline level. The primary psychotropic drug was some form of stimulants (26 percent). To exacerbate the matter, 17 percent were on psychotropic cocktails. Over the course of the study, the number of those who were consistently taking psychotropic drugs increased from 40 percent to 52 percent.[6]

The aforementioned numbers only paint a superficial portrait of

---

[6] R.E. Mattison, "Use of Psychotropic Medications in Special Education Students with Serious Emotional Disturbance," *Journal of Child and Adolescent Psychopharmacology* 9.3 (1999): 149-155.

the systemic issues at play in this dynamic. There are so many different platforms to examine in order to paint a panoramic view that it will be impossible to present a comprehensive portrait here; even so, it is important to, at least, take a look at some of the major factors involved. Any time pharmaceutical grade medications (and I used the word "medications" very lightly, because the truth is that they are simply legalized drugs) are involved, we are talking about the involvement of Big Pharma. When Big Pharma is involved, the bottom line is always profit, not healing. Right now the prescribing of psychotropic drugs to young black boys is a $50 billion per year industry.

The black population in this country has also represented a high profit margin for businesses, whether it has been as slaves providing free labor, sharecroppers providing virtually free labor or as low-income workers providing high productivity at low cost wages. Both the Private Prison Industrial Complex and Special Education systems have produced mechanisms in which the black man will continue to be exploited for the sake of profit. The continuity of the system is quite fluid, meaning that young black men diagnosed with behavioral and learning disabilities, who are prescribed psychotropic drugs are more likely to find themselves in the prison system.

There is currently a lot of discussion coming primarily from the bootstrap faction that points to the fact that everyone has choices, and the fact that more than 40 percent of the male prison population is made up of African Americans is the result of choice.[7] This argument is made on a basis that is completely superficial—ignoring all of the major factors, such as poverty, mis-education, disenfranchisement and

---

[7] Wikipedia, "Statistics of Incarcerated African American Males," Wikipedia.org, https://en.wikipedia.org/wiki/Statistics_of_incarcerated_African-American_males (accessed June 23, 2015).

marginalization of black men, just to name a few. One aspect of the complex equation that leads so many black men to experience incarceration at some point in their lives is their treatment within the special education system.

According to an investigative report by Katherine Stapp, African American children, especially boys are at a much higher risk of being diagnosed as having ADHD—by far the most commonly diagnosed condition among elementary aged students. At the same time that the risk of being diagnosed with ADHD has increased, the exposure to effective treatment options has not. The most common method of treatment has been the prescription of some type of psychotropic drug. In the case of ADHD, the most commonly prescribed drug is methylphenidate, also known as Ritalin. Although Ritalin is classified as a stimulant, it generally has a reverse effect on those individuals who suffer from hyperactivity. The problem here is the same as with any pharmaceutical drug: it is designed to address the symptoms rather than the cause. A greater concern is the fact that the potential side effects of Ritalin are extreme.

Allow me to put things into proper perspective for you. It is easy to view psychotropic drugs, such as Adderall, Ritalin, Concerta, Vyvanse and Focalin, as harmless drugs that help young hyperactive children focus; still, what has to be understood is that the Controlled Substances Act, which is monitored by the Drug Enforcement Administration, classifies these drugs as Schedule II drugs, meaning that they have very little medical uses and they are highly addictive. Think about this for a minute; we are giving consent for our children, as young as five years old, to be given drugs that are mind-altering chemicals and extremely addictive, and yet we wonder why there is a drug problem in our communities. Now the dynamic surrounding the drug epidemic in Black America is far more complex than the existence of the psychotropic drug war on young black boys, but this element cannot be ignored.

To paint a more lucid portrait of the dangers associated with Ritalin, it is classified as a Schedule II drug, meaning that it is as addictive as heroin and cocaine. In fact, Ritalin is one molecule off from being cocaine, and it affects the brain in exactly the same manner as cocaine. Some of the side effects of Ritalin and other stimulant use are insomnia, loss of appetite and increased heart rate. There are studies available that reveal that long-term Ritalin use can lead to certain forms of heart disease and premature death, and yet this is a drug that is frequently prescribed to our young boys. Doesn't it seem somewhat ironic that this nation has been fighting a 45 year war on drugs that has been predominantly fought in black communities, while at the same time doctors are legally prescribing the same drugs to our young black boys.

According to Rhonda Carlos Smith of the Black Child Development Institute, black children are highly over-represented in the majority of systems as being at risk.[8] According to studies, something as simple as overcrowding—a major issue in inner-city schools—can create a situation in which an inappropriate amount of energy is expended by teachers to maintain control over their classroom. This type of environment exacerbates the disruptive behavior of some students. The default solution for this has been to designate the student with a behavioral or learning disability and assign them to special education. What is of greater concern, is the fact that black children, especially boys, are referred to early intervention programs at a much higher rate than others.

---

[8] Katherine Stapp, *Black Children Often Mislabeled as Hyperactive* (Inter Press Service Agency, 2014).

Dr. Janice Hutchinson, a child psychiatrist, emphasizes the fact that all hyperactivity is not ADHD. She points to the fact that issues such as stress, abuse or depression can all manifest themselves in some form of inattentiveness. This again goes to the core issue of not addressing the source or cause of the problem. Imagine a child that may be suffering from abuse being drugged so that he can pay attention in school or so that his teacher can be more effective in her work. It seems that everyone except the student is being considered in this equation.

Ritalin is not the only psychotropic drug being used to wage war on our children. Drugs such as Adderall, Vyvanse, Concerta, Zoloft and Paxil are other common psychotropic drugs that are being given to our children as early as five years old.

I think it is also important to point out the fact that all of these diagnoses are not scientifically based. They are based on the opinion of school psychologists who basically get paid to funnel our children into the special education system.

A closer observation of the special education system and the various titles that are disproportionately assigned to our children will reveal a systematic development of conditions that are created for the purpose of providing an explanation for the natural resistance to an oppressive and hostile system by our children, especially our boys. The American education system is not designed to foster the natural masculinity in boys of any race or nationality, but it institutes a higher level of assault on black masculinity, because it fears the power that black masculinity represents.

We must be careful not to become complicit in the systematic feminization of our young boys, who are our future leaders.

It was Carter G. Woodson that presented the fact that the process of education, inside and outside of the school system, is a significant part of the process of creating the capacity to control a man's thoughts, thereby controlling his actions. Let's take a look at what he had to say on the matter:

> If you can control a man's thinking, you do not have to worry about his actions. When you determine what a man shall think, you do not have to concern yourself about what he will do. If you make a man feel that he is inferior, you do not have to compel him to accept an inferior status, for he will seek it for himself. If you make a man think that he is justly an outcast, you do not have to order him to the back door. He will go without being told; and if there is no back door, his very nature will demand one.[9]

A man can only think along the lines of his formulated thought processes, which constitute a part of his developmental process. This means that the information that is inculcated[10] into the mind and psyche of an individual, especially during those formative years, has an immense impact on their decision-making capacity. The collective thinking of blacks is not some phenomenon that cannot be explained, it is a direct result of mis-education, or more lucidly, misinformation. We have been lied to about who we are, and we have collectively accepted the lie as truth—to the point that when someone stands up to challenge the lie, many of us will defend it.

A significant part of this lie is perpetuated through the public education system; however, it does not end there. In fact, the public education system only serves to reinforce what many of us are feeding

---

[9] Carter G. Woodson, *The Mis-Education of the Negro* (Tribeca Books, 1933).

[10] Inculcated: to teach and impress by frequent repetitions or admonitions: indoctrinated.

our own children in regular doses. Far too often, I have witnessed black parents reinforcing erroneous concepts and images of who we are to their children. Far too often, I have heard the black mother, in a fit of rage, yell—you are not ever going to be anything but sorry. Self-hatred has metastasized from within the black community. The information that we are providing our youth is conditioning them to believe that they are justly outcasts, and we consistently send them messages that they have no power, leaving them to believe that they must depend upon the oppressor for their livelihood.

Make no mistake about it, it is our responsibility to educate and inform our children about who they are, and where they come from, but first, we must gain a lucid perspicacity of who we are. We must shake the faulty paradigms of inferiority and impotence in order to embrace our inherent power. We must fill our minds with the truth of our history and heritage, while relinquishing the images of European superiority. It is the acquiescence to white supremacy that provides its power, and blacks must learn how to resist empowering the system that is diametrically opposed to our advancement. We can no longer be complicit in our own oppression and destruction.

I will even argue that we must relinquish the concept of equality, because we are the only group seeking it. Every other group is seeking dominance. As long as equality is the goal, we will always come in behind those who seek to be at the top of the order. Our goal must be to rise to the pinnacle of our design—nothing less. I challenge each of you to make it your passion to know who you are and make it your ministry to teach our youth.

The genius of the current caste system, and what most distinguishes it from its predecessors, is that it appears voluntary. People choose to commit crimes, and that's why they are locked up or locked out, we are told. This feature makes the politics of responsibility particularly tempting, as it appears the system can be avoided with good behavior. But herein lies the trap. All people make mistakes. All of us are sinners. All of us are criminals. All of us violate the law at some point in our lives. In fact, if the worst thing you have ever done is speed ten miles over the speed limit on the freeway, you have put yourself and others at more risk of harm than someone smoking marijuana in the privacy of his or her living room. Yet there are people in the United States serving life sentences for first-time drug offenses, something virtually unheard of anywhere else in the world.

Michelle Alexander
The New Jim Crow:
Mass Incarceration
in the Age of Colorblindness
2010

Chapter 4

Mass Incarceration and the Private Prison Industrial Complex

The mis-education of young black children has a direct correlation between the high dropout rate of young black boys and the mass incarceration of young black men.[1] The public education system, especially special education, has been used as a staging ground and preparatory process for preparing young black men for prison. Although recent years have shown some improvement in the high school graduation rate of black males, it is important to understand that there is still a long way to go. It is also important to understand that graduating from a system that is designed to marginalize your creativity and expressive power is not necessarily a good thing. However, we do understand that a young black man who graduates from high school does reduce his risk of becoming incarcerated at some point in his life.

Being a native of Texas, the birthplace of the Private Prison Industrial Complex, I have had the opportunity to observe this phenomenon up close and personal. In order to effectively battle this monster, we must be able to see it for what it is. We must understand that blacks were brought to this country for the purpose of providing free labor in order to maximize profit. The Emancipation Proclamation, in no way, changed this, it simply changed the industrial process through

---

[1] Simon McCormack, "Black Men Who Dropped out of High School Have Very High Risk of Going to Prison: Study," *Huffington Post*, http://www.huffingtonpost.com/2014/05/07/black-men-dropped-out-prison-rate_n_5276090.html (accessed June 24, 2015).

which it would be effectively carried out. Slavery was replaced with convict leasing programs, which were the precursor to the Private Prison Industrial Complex.

Private prisons have become so popular within this nation's free-enterprise system that they are now being traded publicly on the stock market. In states like Texas, where inmates are still not paid wages for their labor, there is a huge push to erect even more private prisons to benefit from the free labor; however, in states in which inmates must receive paid wages for their labor, the wages are significantly lower than the minimum wage among free citizens, making prison labor highly profitable.

The private industrial complex is actually the progeny of an industrialized world in which black manual labor has been replaced by automation and the shipping of manual labor jobs to third-world countries. The jobs that were not shipped to third-world countries were moved out of black communities, with many of them being repurposed for prison labor at a fraction of the cost of operating a business in the free world. Inmates across this nation are producing everything from textiles to automotive parts, driving profits through the roof.

The problem is not only in the use of prison labor, but it lies in the necessity to ensure that the occupancy at these private prisons does not fall below 85 percent. Whenever these occupancies fall below 85 percent, the government has to pay a penalty. So, in order to avoid these penalties there has been an over-criminalization of a specific group—the group that was initially intended to provide the free and cheap labor in this nation—the black man. So the black man has been targeted and isolated with the prison population in mind.

Although the CIA has never openly admitted that it intentionally flooded black neighborhoods with drugs for the purpose of destroying them, it did admit that it intentionally blocked law enforcement efforts to investigate and stop illegal drug networks that were helping to fund the covert war it was managing in Nicaragua. Although there has never been an admission of the intent to criminalize the black man and to destroy the core of the black community, there is plenty of ammunition to fuel the theories of many conspiracy theorists that suggest drugs have been used as a weapon of genocide when it comes to blacks, such as the fact that the drug crisis that appeared in the black community did not appear until after the War on Drugs was officially declared.

The truth is that the War on Drugs actually began at a time when drug use in the black community was on a decline. What did result from the declaration of the War on Drugs was a steep increase in arrests and convictions for drug offenses. What is even more telling is the fact that there was, and still is, a huge disparity in sentencing between white men and black men for the same crimes. Since the War on Drugs began, the prison population has completely exploded—going from approximately 300,000 to more than 2 million, with the vast majority of this increase being men of color. The current U.S. prison population completely towers over all other industrialized nations in the world. This is true, even when countries like China, Iran and Russia are thrown into the equation.

What is also important is the fact that it is these large privately owned prison corporations that are spending billions lobbying federal and state legislatures for harsher penalties on crimes—serving to increase the stays of inmates.

ELUCIDATING THE DIFFERENCE BETWEEN DROPOUT AND GRADUATION RATES

It is not uncommon for people to play with statistics in a manner that allows them to place greater emphasis on a specific point that they are trying to make; yet, I believe it is important to create a high level of lucidity when it comes to understanding the dropout rate of young black males.

To keep the explanation brief and to avoid the highly technical aspect of statistical data, I will venture to simplify the explanation in lay terms. When research is being done to determine graduation rates, researchers simply divide the number of graduates by the number of students enrolling in high school four years prior.

The dropout rate is not the remainder, because there are a number of different factors that play into the equation. Just because a student did not graduate in four years does not mean that they dropped out. It could mean that they were retained or they may have even graduated a year earlier, consequently affecting that year's statistics. When estimating dropout rates, researchers take the number of 16 through 24-year-olds in the U.S. who withdrew from grades 10 through 12 in the last 12 months.[2] As you can see, a high dropout rate does not necessarily reflect a corresponding graduation rate. The statistics would have the public believe that the vast majority of black males are not graduating, and it is simply not that simple. On the other hand, it is important to realize that there is a problem with black males dropping out and the direct correlation with a heightened risk of becoming incarcerated. According to a recent report by the Brookings Institution's

---

[2] Ivory Toldson, "Think You Know the Dropout Rates for Black Males? You're Probably Wrong," *The Root*, http://www.theroot.com/articles/culture/2014/06/dropout_rates_for_black_males_are_misleading_and_wrong.html (accessed June 24, 2015).

Hamilton Project, black male dropouts that were born in 1975 have a 75 percent chance of going to prison at some point in their life.[3]

THE SCHOOL TO PRISON PIPELINE

When I first began to examine the complex dynamics of the mis-education of black youth in America, I was bombarded with a multiplicity of elements that were, in one way, inextricably bound, but in another way, they were completely autonomous entities. The mass incarceration of black men is nothing new. Since the quasi-liberation of black slaves in the 1860s, there has been a progressive plan in play that is designed to manage, manipulate and exploit blacks through a systematic collective medium. The mass incarceration of black men in America is one element of the contemporary perpetuation of America's latest racist caste—creating a distinct stratification[4] of the American population along the lines of wealth, social status and race.

It is important for blacks to be able to see and understand the pattern of racism in this country, in order to effectively devise a viable plan of defeating it. From slavery to Jim Crow, segregation on up to the contemporary system of racism, blacks have been systematically oppressed and exploited to ensure the power and stability of the white wealthy elite. While protecting the wealthy elite, this system inherently provides an exceptional level of privilege for all whites—from everything to greater opportunities in business and the job market to something as simple as a greater sense of self.

Using the school system as a staging ground for the categorization of blacks was highly strategic, and it has proven to be highly effective.

[3] McCormack, "Black Men Who Dropped out of High School Have Very High Risk of Going to Prison."

[4] Stratification: the result of stratifying: to form, deposit, or arrange in strata.

While we have many self-proclaimed gurus who like to talk about freedom of choice, the truth is the education system is effectively presenting an image to black students that is reflective of limited choices. Those who don't drop out of high school and put themselves at risk for prison are conditioned to be a part of the corporate plantation, where they work to help fulfill the dreams of others. The current public education system does not prepare black children for success—not when success is defined as achieving the capacity to function in financial and creative autonomy.

The greatest problem still remains to be the fact that this system has found a way to alienate and disenfranchise our young boys. Generally speaking, there are three primary goals that white supremacy desires to accomplish through the mis-education of our black youth:

- To create a strong sense of self-hatred by reinforcing the inferiority complex that is currently existing in the minds of a significant number of blacks.
- To foster white love—causing blacks to place everything white on a pedestal while despising anything black
- To effeminize the black male and the black male image. This goes as far as homosexualizing young black boys. If we study this even closer, we will see that there is an agenda to even promote homosexual supremacy in the black community, especially when it comes to our men.

When a young black boy is resistant to these vices, he is labeled as having behavioral disorders, such as oppositional defiant disorder—initiating a process of drugging and alienation that drives the child further and further away.

At the same time that this is taking place, there is also the criminalization of young black boys in motion. The age at which young black boys are introduced into the criminal justice system is getting lower and lower each year. Offenses that would have drawn detention, or at the worst, suspension, now result in expulsion and/or arrest. Once a child has been introduced to the criminal justice system, their lives are changed forever. They will face obstacles and challenges that will increase the level of difficulty that they are already facing in life. A 2014 study revealed that nearly 50 percent of all black men in the U.S. under the age of 23 have been arrested at least once.[5] What is interesting is that this number almost perfectly corresponds with the number of black males that fail to graduate with their appropriate year group.

While so many people speak about the power of choice, which I agree with in its proper context, we are witnessing a systematic assault on our young black men that ensures that by the time they reach adulthood the odds have been disproportionately stacked against them.

The herding of black men into the prison system does not stop with the arrest. There are numbers that reveal that black men are arrested at a much higher rate than their white counterparts for the same crimes, although research reveals that white men are committing these crimes at an equal rate. Also, black men are more likely to be stopped and searched for drugs, although white men are actually more likely to have drugs on them. To exacerbate the matter, black men are sentenced more harshly for the same crimes.

Michelle Alexander did a remarkable job in bringing this specific mechanism of racism to light in her book, *The New Jim Crow: Mass Incarceration in the Age of Color Blindness*. Alexander points to the bur-

---

[5] Gary Younge, "The Routine Criminalization of Young Black Men is a Nation's Shame," *Alternet*, http://www.alternet.org/news-amp-politics/criminalization-young-black-men-abomination (accessed June 23, 2015).

den of carrying the title of convicted felon in America. She points to the fact that once an inmate is released, they are denied their right to vote, excluded from juries and generally relegated to a subordinated and segregated racial existence.[6]

The mass incarceration of black men also helps to perpetuate the cycle of poverty in the black community. Alexander systematically develops a lucid portrait of the organized methodology that economically and psychologically castrates the black male. There are laws, regulations and rules in place that are systematically reinforced by social stigma. These laws serve to bar the former inmate from participating in the mainstream economy—minimizing their ability to obtain housing, employment or public benefits.

The public education system can be accurately viewed as a system that is rapidly evolving into the number one referral source of young black men into the Private Prison Industrial Complex. The numbers are clear, any young black man who falls victim to mis-education and special education will find themselves at higher risk to become consumed by the snares that have been set by political and corporate arms that are functioning as the mechanisms that work to ensure that there is a steady flow of young black able bodies to maintain the required capacity of the Private Prison Industrial Complex.

Keep in mind that it has always been the purpose for blacks to provide free or cheap labor, and once slaves were freed the focus of white supremacy America was to systematically exterminate blacks, and this has taken place in a number of ways, with the primary method being abortion. However, another effective method for controlling and reducing the black population is to reduce the capacity of the

---

[6] Michelle Alexander, *The New Jim Crow: Mass Incarceration in the Age of Color Blindness* (New York: The New Press, 2010).

black male to reproduce, and this is effectively carried out by incarcerating them. Not only does it influence those who are incarcerated, but it also negatively impacts the subsequent generation, because they are automatically placed at a higher risk to become incarcerated and to live a life of poverty.

THE CRIMINALIZATION OF THE BLACK MALE

There is a systemic widespread assumption concerning young black men in America. This assumption is that black men are naturally more prone to violence and crime. It leads to a disproportionate level of fear and an overreaction by law enforcement personnel. The issues that surround this phenomenon are quite complex, but they lead to an unfair stigmatization of black men. It is important to understand that this natural assumption is not by accident. It is the result of the systematic criminalization of black men.

This act of criminalizing black men through various mechanisms, especially the propaganda that is created and distributed through mass media, is a focused effort to provide the justification for the murder, mistreatment and mass incarceration of black men. You can see this same modality used by Adolf Hitler in the propaganda campaign that was used to villainize and dehumanize the Jews. The less human and more threatening a specific group may seem, the less resistance there will be when this group of people is slaughtered, marginalized and incarcerated. This is why there is no outcry on behalf of young black men being systematically slaughtered by white police officers. There is a general consensus that black men are violent, and therefore dangerous; therefore, justifying the act of so many white cops shooting black men dead, while proclaiming that they fear for their lives and safety. It seems to me that we have far too many scary police officers on the job.

When more than $24,000.00 per year is spent to house each inmate, while only $8,000.00 is spent to educate young black boys, there should be no surprise that there is a perpetual pipeline that leads from the back door of schools to the front door of prisons.

It is many of these assumptions concerning black males that lead white teachers, especially white female teachers to assume that their black male students will have behavior problems and learning disabilities. It is these type of postulations that lend to the eventual categorization and the designation of special education tags for a disproportionate number of black boys.

To paint a lucid portrait of just what our men are facing, I want to share a story of a young black man from Philadelphia—Darrin Manning.[7] Manning is an honor roll student from Philadelphia, who was chased down and assaulted by cops, and ultimately had a female cop frisk him with such force that she ruptured his testicle. Manning was sixteen at the time. However, to truly understand the criminalization of black men, you must view this incident while framed in its proper context.

Manning and some of his high school basketball teammates were exiting a Philadelphia subway on the way to a basketball game. It was so cold, that the boys' principal had given them hats, gloves and scarves to wear. As they exited the subway, they noticed several police officers who were "staring them down," and Manning suggests that one of the officers may have said something smart. The police involved say that they saw a dozen young men running in "ski masks," so they gave chase. The truth is that they were not wearing ski masks, they were

---

[7] Sebastian Murdock, "Pa. Teen, Allegedly Has Testicle Ruptured By Cop," *Huffington Post*, http://www.huffingtonpost.com/2014/01/23/darrin-manning-testicle-rupture_n_4651700.html (accessed June 24, 2015).

wearing ski caps. While the other boys ran, Manning determined that running implied guilt, so he stopped.

According to Manning, he had not done anything wrong, but he was tackled by the police. During this initial accosting by the police, Manning says that a female officer frisked him so ferociously that he ended up having to have emergency surgery to repair a ruptured testicle.

Police claimed that Manning hit an officer several times although there were no injuries to corroborate the claim. Nevertheless, Manning was charged with assaulting an officer and resisting arrest. There were numerous eyewitnesses on the scene that corroborate Manning's account of the police using excessive force.

What happened to Darrin Manning was simply the manifestation of the criminalization of young black men. Much in the same way that Trayvon Martin was targeted without cause—ultimately costing him his life—Manning was targeted for no other reason than the fact that he was black. There is a widespread assumption that any group of young black men that are hanging out together must be up to no good.

The emasculation of black men in America has often been used as a metaphorical expression that explains the constant assault on the masculinity and power of black men; however, in this particular case, it is both figurative and literal. Manning's doctors are not certain of whether this young man will ever be able to father children as a result of this incident.

This particular incident, like so many like it, presents many issues and questions. Since when does wearing a ski mask—which they were not—in freezing cold weather constitute a crime? This incident provides a lucid explanation of why so many parents are perplexed concerning what to tell their children about encounters with the police. When consideration is given to what happened to Darrin Manning, it is hard to tell your children not to run from the cops. Not only is there a chance of physical harm, but there is a greater chance that they will end up in the criminal justice system. There is a routine criminalization of young black men in America that exceeds anything that can be considered a statistical aberration, reaching more into the realm of a systematic abomination. The United States has more people imprisoned now than did the Soviet Union during the gulag, and more than 40 percent of the prison population are made up of black men.

According to Think Progress.org, the United States not only has the largest prison population per capita, but it has the overall largest prison population by number and percentage in the entire world. Black men represent a highly disproportionate number of the U.S. prison population, and that is by design.[8]

Darrin Manning's mother's response to the incident brings a great deal of illumination to just how dark things have become: "I'm just grateful that they didn't just kill him."

This statement speaks volumes in so many ways. What type of society are we living in where a mother whose son has been mutilated by those who took an oath to protect him, and her response is that she is simply grateful that he is alive? Unfortunately, this does not only speak to the darkness of the times as far as the infliction of racist machinations upon blacks, but it also speaks to the defeatist mindset of blacks who have taken on a just survive mentality.

---

[8] Nicole Flatow, "The United States Has The Largest Prison Population in the World—and It's Growing," *Think Progress*, http://thinkprogress.org/justice/2014/09/17/3568232/the-united-states-had-even-more-prisoners-in-2013/ (accessed June 24, 2015).

To create an even stronger context to this story, and more importantly, this issue of criminalizing black men. When this story initially took place, there was a great emphasis placed on the remarkable character and accomplishments of this young exceptional student. And while the accomplishments of Darrin Manning are remarkable, they should not be used as a determining factor of whether or not these white police officers were justified in profiling, assaulting and mutilating him. Raving about the fact that he was an "A" student with such a promising future lends to the postulation and the mindset that the "C" student, or the child with a troubled past, could somehow be deserving of this sort of treatment by law enforcement. The truth is that they should not be allowed to do that to any child under any circumstance. He was unarmed and he did not pose a threat. He is sure to have psychological scars, and it is possible that he will be physically impacted for the remainder of his life because this nation has chosen to criminalize its young men of color and give its law enforcement personnel carte blanche to attack, mutilate and kill young black men at their discretion.

Although accentuating the good character of the victim may be a great individual strategy, it does not serve us well on a broader scale, because it allows the media to criminalize kids like Trayvon Martin and Michael Brown. Trayvon Martin shooting the middle finger on YouTube or Michael Brown allegedly strong-arming some cigars in no way justifies their murders. They were no more deserving of what happened to them than Darrin Manning.

Actually, the point being made here is far less esoteric than it may appear at first glance. With more than 50 percent of young black men under the age of 23 having an arrest record, it is apparent that there is a systematic force at play to drive them toward the Private Prison

Industrial Complex—placing them at greater risk of being murdered by cops in the process.

It is our responsibility to effectively engage this issue. One of the first things that we must do is to engage our responsibility of educating and preparing our youth for success in a system that is hostile towards them. We must also begin the process of building and owning our own, which will allow us to provide greater insulation and protection for our progeny. The less we expose them to this system, the less damage that can be done.

We have to give up this mindset that our enemies can be trusted, and we must abandon the almost inherent need to be accepted by them. We must be willing to shift the importance assigned to everything white to the building of everything black.

VEILED RACISM: THE PRIVATE PRISON INDUSTRIAL COMPLEX

The term "Private Prison Industrial Complex" is an expression that is used to attribute the massive and rapid expansion of the inmate population in the United States to the powerful political influence of privately owned prison companies, as well as to those businesses that directly profit from this complex, such as the companies that supply goods and services to these institutions. This industrial conglomerate is large and highly lucrative.

These private companies that make up the prison complex have successfully lobbied for stricter sentencing laws that extend the amount of time that can be passed down for certain crimes. To ensure their profit margins, these companies also require federal and state governments to guarantee a minimum annual capacity. Due to the substantial penalty of not meeting this minimum, the government has developed laws that have served to increase the national incarceration rate. Currently the U.S. has, by far, the largest prison population in the world amongst industrialized countries.

There is a complex dynamic at play as far as the imprisonment of American citizens. There is the inevitable need to feed the machine, meaning that there must be a constant flow of inmates. Additionally, white supremacy must find a way to effectively manage the black population. As the influx of illegal immigrants from the south continues, the country is establishing a new working class—meaning that the need for blacks as the permanent lower class is rapidly diminishing. This will ultimately force the black low-income workers out of the job market and into a deeper level of poverty.

One of the inherent side effects of poverty is an increased crime rate. Since 1980, this country has experienced a steady and sharp incline in the number of African American men who are incarcerated, creating a situation in which the prison population is not demographically reflective of the general population. What is transpiring is the transition of blacks from the lowest level of the working class to the primary population of the Private Prison Industrial Complex.

As I stated, the dynamic here is extremely complex, and we must be careful not to place too much emphasis on one particular element of this massive scheme. As much as we must acknowledge the presence of racism in the grand scheme of things, it is not the only thing that fuels this profit machine. The fallacious philosophies through which many of the problematic issues that plague those who are ensconced in poverty creates the foundation for this massive machine. The immediate response to many of the social issues that are inextricably connected to poverty is imprisonment. This is because the vast majority of these issues are veiled and conveniently grouped under one all-encompassing category—crime!

We must understand that an asserted effort has been made by white supremacy to ensure that the black population remains poor. This is confirmed and validated through the fact that on the eve of the civil war, quasi-free blacks owned only one-half of one percent of this nation's wealth. Here we are 150 years later, and blacks still only own one-half of one percent of this nation's wealth.[9] Only through a systematic process could this occur.

Where there is poverty, there will be crime. The problem is that many people, even those who are being negatively impacted by this system, believe that imprisonment is the answer; however, the truth is that imprisonment does not make any of these problems disappear, it only serves to make people disappear. In our case, the vast majority of those whom the system is causing to disappear is the black male population. Actually, not only does this flow not help mitigate the problems created by poverty; it serves to exacerbate them. When you remove men from the community at the rate in which black men are being extracted from inner-city communities, you leave a void of leadership, protection, covering and role models. This type of policy leaves mothers to attempt to execute the role of both parents, which is impossible. Despite the fact that this type of policy does not work to eliminate the issues surrounding poverty, the fact that herding people who are a part of marginalized communities into prisons has become highly profitable, and it ensures that the cycle will continue.

The Private Prison Industrial Complex provides the answer to the dilemma of what will be done with the black man. The black man poses a constant and consistent threat to the power structure of white supremacy, and the Private Prison Industrial Complex provides the

[9] Anderson, *Black Labor, White Wealth.*

immediate solution to the problem. In the meantime, white-owned private companies are generating enormous profits off of the backs of black men. What we are experiencing is simply the latest form of slavery.

While many will argue that crime is a choice, which I agree with, I must also present the fact that the deck has been stacked and the choices have been reduced tremendously. There is no shortage of studies that reveal that crime is a direct result of poverty. There are only three ways that a man can support his family:

1. Through income generated from a job or business

2. By receiving supplemental support through government social programs

3. Crime

According to the Fact Tank, the unemployment rate for blacks is consistently twice that of whites in this country.[10] The disparity is even worse when comparing white men and black men. A recent article by Al Jazeera America revealed that while the unemployment rate for white men is actually 4.4 percent, the unemployment rate for black men is nearly three times that—reaching its peak of 19 percent in 2010. Keep in mind that the unemployment numbers only reflect those who are currently working through government employment channels looking for work or unemployment compensation. This means that the unemployment rate for black men is actually much higher.

The truth is that social programs are not available for men who wish to stay with and support their family. The social programs that

[10]Drew Desilver, "Black Unemployment Rate is Consistently Twice That of Whites," *Pew Research Center*, http://www.pewresearch.org/fact-tank/2013/08/21/through-good-times-and-bad-black-unemployment-is-consistently-double-that-of-whites/ (accessed June 24, 2015).

were introduced in the late 1960s predominantly required that no man be living in the home of any woman receiving benefits—creating a break in the black family nucleus as blacks struggled to deal with the growing unemployment rate. Ironically, this growth in unemployment in the late 1960s can be directly traced to the process of integration, since when blacks gave up ownership of their businesses, they also relinquished their power to hire and support other blacks. This placed blacks at the mercy of the white economy.

That leaves crime as the only other viable option to generate revenue. However, before blacks put on their victim's jacket, it is important to point out that if we are victims, we are victims of our own failures. We have failed to see the power in ownership. We failed to see the fallibility in integration. We constantly fail to see the dangers of trusting a white educational system to educate our youth. Right now, we are sinking in the quicksand of our own failures. This is not to marginalize the pernicious attacks of white supremacy racism, but it is to illuminate the fact that despite their attacks, we are still in a position of power to determine how we will respond. Our compliance is what has provided white supremacy with its power. If we are to effectively engage this vehement struggle for empowerment in an efficacious manner, it begins with taking back the responsibility of educating our progeny. We must establish the paradigms through which they view life.

The public education system is a staging ground that prepares our young black boys for a life of incarceration, and it creates the foundation for a life of poverty and frustration for our black girls. Even those who successfully navigate through this system are not guaranteed success within the grand scheme of the white supremacy structure. According to a recent article in the New York Times, finding employment after graduating college for blacks is a tougher road to travel than it is for whites.[11] Additionally, a study conducted by the University of Chicago Booth School of Business revealed that applicants with white sounding names were 50 percent more likely to be called for an interview than applicants with black sounding names but equal credentials.

BLACK GENOCIDE IN AMERICA

There has been a great deal of discussion concerning black genocide in America as of late. While browsing my news feed on Facebook this morning, I came across a post that brought pause to my rapidly cycling thought process. In essence, the post was asserting that the killing of young black men on the streets of America is a completely different war than the 1,800 black lives lost to abortion every day. Although I can understand the reasoning behind the argument, the postulation is highly fallible.[12]

The person who was making the statement was attempting to effectively engage the attempt of white supremacy America and all of its sycophants to justify, or at least, marginalize the deaths of young black men at the hands of white police officers across this nation. Honestly, this dilemma has to be addressed, and one does not excuse the other.

It is common protocol for the powers that be to use what is known as "logical fallacy" to disrupt the flow of lucid truth. Abortion, in no way, justifies the senseless slaughter of black men at the hands of police

---

[11] Patricia Cohen, "For Recent Black College Graduates, a Tougher Road to Employment," *New York Times*, http://www.nytimes.com/2014/12/25/business/for-recent-black-college-graduates-a-tougher-road-to-employment.html?_r=0 (accessed June 24, 2015).

[12] Marianne Bertrand, "Racial Bias in Hiring," *Chicago GSB | Capital Ideas*. The University of Chicago Graduate School of Business, 2003. http://www.chicagobooth.edu/capideas/spring03/racialbias.html (accessed June 10, 2014).

officers; but the powers that be are using it, much in the manner in which they attempt to use the violence perpetuated against blacks by other blacks—"black on black" crime—as a means to mitigate the negative actions of white police officers.

ELUCIDATING THE DILEMMA

What is important in gaining a functional perspicacity of this multiplicity of genocidal methods is the fact that it is all different means for the purpose of achieving one common goal. In essence, it is multitudinous battles fought on numerous fronts, but it is one war. We are in the midst of a war in which the enemy seeks our ultimate demise. Whether it is the Private Prison Industrial Complex, the senseless slaughter of our men in the streets by cops, or the passive—yet deadliest approach—of abortion, it all works toward the end game of the total annihilation of the black race.

What we must really watch is the sleight-of-hand that white supremacy has become extremely astute at performing. When you consider that two black men are killed by police officers every week in this country, one every 28 hours if you consider security guards and other authoritative positions, the number may seem staggering at first until you juxtapose that statistic with the abortion numbers. Abortion robs the black community of 1,876 hundred lives per day across this nation. It can be easily hypothesized that the murder of black men by police officers is a diversionary tactic to draw attention away from areas in which significantly greater damage is being done.

This does not mean that we should dismiss or ignore what is happening to our men in the street. It simply means that we must be prepared to fight the war on all fronts.

THE HISTORY OF ABORTION IN THE BLACK COMMUNITY

The high number of abortions in the black community is not a coincidence. To understand the elemental dynamics at play here, you must have an understanding of its origin. All of this is the work of Margaret Sanger, the founder of Planned Parenthood; however, it was not originally called Planned Parenthood. The organization was initially known as the American Birth Control League, and then in 1939, it changed its name to the Birth Control Federation of America. The primary focus of this organization was its Negro Project. This project was designed to, at the very least, restrict the growth of the black population, but many believe that it was designed to exterminate it.

The plan was implemented with great precision and cleverness. One of the cleverest mechanisms used by Sanger was the beguilement of the black elite, the well-educated and economically affluent blacks, into supporting her scheme. Many of them were enticed to believe that abortion was a way of improving the race and garnering the respect of whites in America.

Sanger even solicited the help of black Christian ministers to help facilitate the implementation of her plan. Below is just one quote where she discusses the importance of utilizing ministers to counter any movement of blacks to rebel against the idea:

> We should hire three or four colored ministers, preferably with social-service backgrounds, and with engaging personalities. The most successful educational approach to the Negro is through a religious appeal. We don't want the word to go out that we want to exterminate the Negro population, and the minister is the man who can straighten out that idea if it ever occurs to any of their more rebellious members.

What makes the Negro Project such a pernicious mechanism is the lasting impact that it has had on the black community. We have become victims of genocide at our own hands.

MALTHUSIAN EUGENICS

Margaret Sanger wisely aligned herself with the prevailing eugenicists of the early 20th century. These eugenicists strongly espoused racial purity and supremacy, especially concerning the Aryan race. Their goal was to purify the Aryan race's bloodlines. This was to be accomplished by encouraging those who were deemed fit to reproduce while restricting the reproduction of the unfit. The ideology was built upon the concept of constraining the inferior races through sterilization, birth control, abortion and segregation.

It is within this context of this ideology that the motive for extermination is exposed. The black dominant gene of people of African descent has the genetic power to completely destroy the white race, which is the result of a recessive gene. In other words, blacks can actually annihilate the whites simply by breeding with them. I have yet to find any work that examines this truth in the distinct manner as *The Isis Papers* by Dr. Francis Cress-Welsing. Her original work, *The Cress Theory of Confrontation* is also a must read on the topic.

Here is another quote from Sanger that clearly points out her primary motive:

> *All children born, beyond what would be required to keep up the population to a desired level, must necessarily perish, unless room is made for them by the death of grown persons. We should facilitate, instead of foolishly and vainly endeavoring to impede, the operations of nature in producing this mortality.*

THE CONTEMPORARY SCHEME

It has been estimated that since 1973 there have been nearly 14 million black fetuses aborted. This can be better understood under the light of statistical data. Although black women—between the ages of 15 to 44 only make up 13 percent of the female population in America, they underwent approximately 36 percent of the abortions.

According to statistics produced by the Alan Guttmacher Institute, black women are five times more likely to have an abortion than white women. On the surface, this may seem coincidental, but a careful examination of the practices of Planned Parenthood reveals something far more cynical. First of all, the vast majority of Planned Parenthood offices are located in or near impoverished neighborhoods that are predominantly occupied by blacks. Second of all, there is a little known policy in which white mothers are counseled by Planned Parenthood to give their children up for adoption in the case of unwanted pregnancies, while black women are almost always encouraged to abort.

Allow me to put the aforementioned numbers into perspective for you. The 14 million lives lost to abortion represents 36 percent growth in the black population that we will never experience. It would have taken our current population of just over 40 million and pushed it to nearly 55 million. This does not take into consideration the progeny that would have been produced by these lost lives.

THE KICKER

If the exorbitant number of lives lost through abortion wasn't enough, there is a backend kicker that totally exacerbates the matter. According to a 1993 Howard University study, African American women over the age of 50 were 4.7 times more likely to develop breast cancer if they had had any abortions in their lives. This is in comparison with black women who had not had abortions.

This information is actually not new. So, not only are lives being destroyed before they ever get started, but a significant amount of the women having these abortions will have their lives prematurely ended by breast cancer.

Make no mistake about this, it is genocide on every front. Does the murder of our young men in the street have any ties to the high rate of abortion in the black community? Absolutely, and attempting to separate the two in order to rationalize our position to those who don't care is not in our best interest. We must recognize the machinations of the enemy and respond with counter measures. We must educate our people, while dealing with the multitudinous issues associated with Post Traumatic Slave Syndrome. We have to find a way to rise above the madness.

This is what happens when an oppressed people are intent upon depending on their oppressors to fund their revolution and elevation. We must take a significant step toward building and owning our own stuff, and this includes the educational process.

No systematic effort toward change has been possible, for, taught the same economics, history, philosophy, literature and religion which have established the present code of morals, the Negro's mind has been brought under the control of his oppressor.

Carter G. Woodson
The Mis-education of the Negro
1933

Chapter 5

Checkmate:
Using Education as the Endgame
Against Blacks in America

The psycho-academic assault on our youth, especially the perni-cious assault on our young boys could literally be a checkmate on the grand chessboard in which this race war is being waged, and one of the greatest dangers for blacks is that they do not even realize that the war is being waged, and that it is being waged at an extremely high level. While blacks are intent on forcing whites to accept us as equals, we are missing the slow, but steady, erosion of every aspect of our her-itage and culture. The black family nucleus has all but been destroyed, and any sense of identity that we have is superficial, lacking the depth to build self-awareness and the power necessary to rise up to live at the level we were designed to live at.

The problem is that blacks have drank the Kool-Aid when it comes to the systematic presentation of the lie that the emancipation proclamation, in some way, implied that whites were ready to co-exist with blacks on an equal plane. Despite the horrors of reconstruction and Jim Crow, we continued to believe that if we simply found ways to assimilate into the system that our adversary would lift their hand of oppression and welcome us into the fold. This was a terrible mis-take. We failed to see the true design and construction of the social hierarchy. Everything in America, and the world for that matter, is built upon economic empowerment. In its simplest form, status and position in this country is not contingent upon intellectual or physiological equality, but it is built upon financial fluidity.

Without economic power, no person or group can possess any type of true influence. When a group or race of people don't have influence, this means that they don't have any real say so in the affairs surrounding their lives. Even when they vote, they will find that they still lack influence, because the elected official will always serve the agenda of those who provide the financial support to ensure that they are able to campaign to remain in office. So, without the financial prowess to invest in the political arena there is no way to influence the laws and policies that directly impact our lives.

While we continue to wage war with picket signs, white supremacy has been systematically removing vital pieces from the chess board, subsequently weakening our overall position, which has never been strong in the first place. This has been done by presenting the illusion of progression while simultaneously diminishing our social, economic and filial strength. Everything that has been a staple of hope for the black community has consistently been under assault. The black family nucleus, which has been the foundation for educating and empowering future generations, has been all but wiped out. As our men have participated in a mass exodus toward white women, and our women have succumbed to the lure of progressive feminism, we have been left in a state of division and weakness—rendering us easy prey.

While we wage an internal war between our men and women, with both pointing the finger at the other, white supremacy has launched an all-out assault against our youth. Using the educational system as a way to weaken our youth and destroy their proclivity to dream big and aspire to greatness.

This assessment of the current situation is not implying that the malevolent assault on Black America cannot be effectively and permanently shut down, but it points to a very precarious situation in which we find ourselves in a position in which we must take action now. We find ourselves in check on the grand chessboard of life. Actually, we have found ourselves in check multitudinous times in the past, and we have always been able to find a way to move out of check; however, this situation is different because we are in check from more than one aspect and the direct assault against our boys could spell our demise, if we lose the masculine influence of black men on a massive scale.

It is important to understand that I am not an advocate of the victim mentality that is so prevalent in black America. I believe in fighting for what you believe and taking what belongs to you; however, one must know what they are fighting against, and that is what this book is about. It is about identifying the strategies of the opposing system and developing counter measures to shut it down. What this means is that, at the end of the day, whether we win or lose is ultimately on us.

This process of mis-education is precarious because the assault is coming from more than one direction. Our men are being incapacitated by the criminal justice system at an alarming rate. They are being shut out of the job market. The public education system is addicting them to psychotropic drugs as early as age five. The quest to feminize or homosexualize the black male image is also taking its toll. If the black male is effectively incapacitated, there is no moving out of check. We will find that we have been successfully checkmated by our adversary.

MEETING THE CHALLENGE: OUR ONLY MOVE

As I stated earlier, checkmate is not yet inevitable, but the window is closing, and there are innumerable impediments that stand in the way of authentic liberation and power. We must first break away from the proclivity to foster divisiveness within our ranks. We must come to the understanding that we will not always agree on everything, but we must understand that without taking collective action, we will be systematically annihilated. We must also refuse to allow things like religion and political ideologies to further divide us. There is one commonality that we will always share, and that is the fact that we are black, meaning that we will always find ourselves in the crosshairs of white supremacy. We must come together based on this commonality and develop strategies that will function to lift us out of the pit of oppression.

The way that we must address this intense assault on our men is to develop a comprehensive and diverse strategy to protect our men, especially our future generations. For instance, we have the power to deal a massive blow to the criminalization and imprisonment of our men by removing our young boys from the public education system and homeschooling them until we can raise the money to erect our own schools. There are a number of homeschooling programs throughout the U.S. that can help parents ensure that they meet all of the requirements.

This action immediately removes our young boys from the direct and negative assaults of the public education system that are designed to cause them to doubt themselves and develop inferiority complexes.

It immediately removes them from the onslaught of psychotropic drugs that are being forced upon them at alarming rates, in which young black boys as young as five years old are on drugs like Zoloft and Ritalin. The chemical imbalances created in the brain by these types of drugs lead to all types of psychoses, which generally contribute to the learning disorders.

Homeschooling also creates a more natural environment for learning—one that is nurturing and safe. When we enroll our children in the public education system, or any school system that is controlled by whites, we expose them to excessive hostility and a conditioning process that teaches them to hate themselves and love their enemies. Far too many blacks in America are using the public school system as a daycare and a baby sitter. The public education system was never meant to be the primary caregiver or the primary conduit through which our children would be educated. This system is not designed to engage the unique and specific needs of our children.

In Africa, parents assume the primary responsibility of educating their children. Even when children are sent off to school to enhance certain academic skills, it is still the parent's responsibility to introduce them to their history. It is their history that helps to form their view of themselves—their self-image. In Visionetics, the study of self-image, parents are considered to be primary label givers.[1] This means that the way that a child views themselves is a direct reflection of the images that are set in the mind of the child by the parent. Although there will be many label givers, including peers and teachers, the role that the parent plays in the process of developing their child's self-image is preeminent, or at least it should be.

When a parent invests themselves in the process of teaching their children their heritage, they help to shape the child's view of themselves. One of the greatest concerns with the current educational

---

[1] Rick Wallace, "The Self-affirming Force of a Christian Self-image," *Straight From the Lab*, 2014.

process through which blacks are informed of their history is that it is limited to the history of this country, which means that the vast majority of black children's view of their history is centered on captivity and oppression. This only serves to foster the feeling of inadequacy—strengthening their inferiority complex.

The truth is that our history goes back much further than that, but it does not serve our oppressors to inform our children of our rich history and the contributions that our ancestors made to civilization. This would serve to elevate their personal self-image, and it would cause them to raise their expectations for themselves. This is why black parents must take the time to create a cognitive notion of greatness in their children before these children are ever exposed to counter-cultural propaganda. When we train our children to expect greatness from themselves, they will receive negative propaganda as something that is diametrically opposed to the personal plan they have established for their own lives, and they will reject and dismiss it.

Also, black parents must unite. The chasm that exists between black women and black men who have children together is huge, and the results are devastating. The black family nucleus was the ideal environment for fostering the positive growth of our children. It contained just the right amount of feminine energy and the ideal amount of masculine energy to ensure that our children had a balanced developmental process. When parents break up, and then determine that the children are a great and powerful weapon to use against their former mate, the ones that suffer most are the children.

We must learn to put our differences as parents aside for the greater good of our children and our race. We must understand that the presence of both parents is essential to the full development of our children. It is time for black parents to understand that our children are not weapons to be used in the process of attempting to reshape or destroy our former mates. They are not to be caught in the center of these narcissistic confrontations that are simply focused on having the last word in a perpetual battle. No person is perfect, and that includes every person that is reading this sentence. With that being understood, you must understand that your mate or former mate will have strengths and weaknesses. It is in the best interest of the child for the parents to work in a manner that maximizes the strengths of each parent, while minimizing the impact of the weaknesses of each.

WE OWN OUR DESTINY

For far too long, we have allowed an external force to write our story. We basically surrendered to the suggestions of white supremacy racism, subsequently taking our queue from them. We have bought into the lie that we are inferior, creating a level of self-hatred that has never existed among any other people in history. We have accepted, without question, the lie that we are helpless to create change, and that we are at the mercy of our oppressor. It is time to understand that white supremacy is absolutely powerless in the absence of black compliance.

BLACK COMPLIANCE IS NOT THE ANSWER TO WHITE SUPREMACY

There has been no shortage of scholarly evidence produced to shed light on the plight of blacks in America. Dr. Francis Cress-Welsing gave us *The Isis Papers*. Dr. Joy DeGruy introduced us to Post Traumatic Slave Syndrome, and Dr. Na'im Akbar provided the blueprint for breaking the psychological tethers associated with slavery. Even with all of the information that is being disseminated by great black minds, I would argue that blacks, as a collective, have not progressed at all.

Recently, I was asked to examine a certain video in which a young black man was appealing to blacks to simply comply with police officers and they would not be at risk of being shot to death. Besides the fact that the assertion he was making was erroneous and unfounded, it revealed another aspect of the black experience in America. It sheds light on a powerful mechanism that has served to keep blacks at the bottom of the socioeconomic pecking order from day one. One of my colleagues was also asked to view the video, and the first thing that he observed was fear.

Although this young black man was speaking from a platform of leadership, he was reacting from a position of fear. His words were expressive of a state of mind that had been conditioned to adapt to the oppressive tactics of the oppressor for the purpose of survival. It has long been the common practice of blacks to conform—to become compliant for the purpose of being accepted and finding peace—yet there has been no peace to be found in compliance. Power only responds to demand, and blacks must come to an understanding that there is a distinct difference between requesting and demanding. Simply put, white supremacy is sustained by the power we, as a race of people, give it.

The compliant and surrendered tone in the voice of this young man in the video was indicative of what has become an inherent response to hostile actions against blacks by whites—relieving the white aggressor of any culpability while shouldering the black victim with the blame. This is the response of a mind that is still in bondage. The psychological chains that held us in place during chattel slavery are still very much intact. We have been freed physically, but the bonds of psychological slavery have proven much more difficult to break.

The man in this video is demonstrating what is known as adaptive survival behavior. Every person has an inherent ability to adapt to their environment for the sake of survival; much of it is instinctive; however, effective adaptation must consider all of the variables. When a group of people and a system created by these people has proven to be consistently hostile without provocation, the group that is under attack must understand that compliance is not the answer. In fact, absolute compliance will only expedite the inevitable.

There have been a number of people who attempted to address this issue, but the points that they were attempting to make were somewhat fuliginous.[2] So, I will use the final paragraphs here to eliminate any nebulosity that I may have created to this point.

As a means of survival, blacks have adopted certain behaviors that are the result of docility and willful compliance. Unfortunately, these adaptive survival behaviors have not proven sufficient in the least. One reason is that we have greatly underestimated our enemy. We assumed that this force that is consistently moving against us desires peace at some level. The truth is that the end game of white supremacy will always be total domination.

Compliance is not the answer. When I speak of non-compliance, it is not the chaotic, disorganized temper tantrums that are common immediately after something happens that we don't like. The non-compliance that I advocate is organized anarchy with an end game of economic empowerment. We don't have to comply with non-black businesses dominating the economic flow in our community. We don't have to comply with the mis-education of our youth, when homeschooling and developing our own education system are

---

[2] Fuliginous: Sooty.

viable options. We don't have to comply with the mistreatment and unfair practices in the workplace when business ownership is an option. When we begin to fight this war with our minds, we will find that we will be faced with fewer instances in which we will be forced to place our bodies at risk.

When I viewed the video of this young man literally begging black people to simply comply, his almost rational-sounding discourse reminded me of something that is a great concern of mine. In a time in which blacks need to be about the tedious task of building our own economic infrastructure on a national level, talks of compliance and peace can be quite distracting to a people that have proven their natural proclivity to acquiesce to the pressure instead of pushing forward.

I don't want any black man or black woman to place themselves in a position in which they could lose their lives at the hand of a police officer. We have sacrificed enough black blood. What I am calling for is for blacks to stand up in unity to move toward a common goal of empowerment. It is important to understand that compliance will not bring peace when the end game of your enemy is complete domination and the total destruction of your people.

We must use the resources and tools that we have at our disposal to work to free the minds of our black brothers and sisters who are still bound to the psychological chains associated with slavery. We must exert great effort to control the messages that our people are receiving. It is time to break those chains.

This means that the greatest accomplishment of white supremacy has been to convince blacks that they have no power. We must be willing to take back our power to live within our purpose as we work toward our destiny. We must understand that no one has absolute power over us. We always have an option, even if that option is to choose death over oppression and bondage. We are where we are because we have failed to take proper action. We have settled into the maze of mediocrity and chosen comfort over character. This is why I say that white supremacy has us in a "check" that could finally produce the checkmate that they have been looking for since the emancipation proclamation.

The assault against our men has weakened our collective leadership, and without male leadership, we are doomed if this doesn't change. Sorry ladies, despite all of the tenets of feminism, no matter how much our women progress, if our men don't survive, our race, as we know it, is doomed. This is why it is vital that we cover our young boys and protect them long enough for them to develop into men who believe in their inherent greatness. This is why the existing men must take ownership of our roles as leaders and providers in our homes and communities.

I will be honest with you. There is not a great deal of fanfare for men who are willing to step into their roles right now, so this means that we must be willing to take on these roles simply because it is our responsibility. Many black women will take a while to come on board, but if we continue to lead from a position of selflessness, they will come on board and they will support our movement.

Now is the moment that we challenge the adversary on the grand chessboard of life. Through proper education of ourselves and our progeny, we not only have the potential to move ourselves out of "check," but we will also find that we have the potential to place our adversary in "check" as well. And history has shown that our adversary does not respond well when they are not the aggressor. In the words of my grandfather: "It ain't no fun when the rabbit has got the gun!" It is time for us to take a more aggressive approach.

AN EXPANDED IMAGE FACILITATES A GREATER VISION

One way that we can help our children is to provide them with expanded imagery—images of the possibilities that lie before them—providing images of greatness and unlimited potential. One way that we can do this is to celebrate greatness within the community. We have to give our children more to aspire to than being a rapper, actor or athlete. There is nothing wrong with either of those professions when a person is willing to master their craft, and they are seeking to dominate their industry; nevertheless, it is immensely important that we expand the imagery to encompass other possibilities that will allow our youth to flow in their natural creativity.

Not everyone is passionate about acting or playing sports, so we must encourage our youth to pursue their passion; but it is imperative that while we are encouraging our children to pursue their passion, that we introduce the imagery that is reflective of what is possible. We must remove the boundaries and parameters that have been set in place for the purpose of limiting their options.

Much in the same way that we celebrate our athletes and actors, we must celebrate the great minds that have mastered sciences and the legal process. We must celebrate our great inventors and innovators. We have to let our children know that there are infinite possibilities when they understand who they really are. At the same time, we must give up our enamored fixation on the accomplishments of whites. We must leave celebrating them up to their own. We cannot be guilty of planting any seed that could sprout up as an inferiority complex. What we are experiencing at this very moment is a self-fulfilling prophesy associated with an inferiority complex that has existed since we arrived here more than 400 years ago. The self-fulfilling prophecy simply points to the fact that when you believe that you are inferior, your behavior will reflect that belief, and all that you will ever accomplish will be rooted in that inferior mindset.

In order to eliminate inferior results that are inextricably bound to the mindset of inferiority, a new paradigm has to be created. This paradigm must be representative of what is possible for black youth, and it must be lucid in its presentation of the innate greatness associated with being black. Personally, I am not one who believes in teaching equality. As an athlete, I have been conditioned to believe that I am greater than my adversary, and the moment that I believe that they are better or even equal, I lose my competitive edge, and my expectation of winning.

In learning this mindset at an early age, I also learned the truth that believing that you are better does not mean that you cannot still respect your opponent—it simply means that you expect to win. I believe that equality is a neutralizing force that breeds the desire to simply be on the same level with the opponent. This is a race, and there will be a winner and a loser, not an equal. I believe that the doctrine of equality is simply another form of compromise that causes blacks to land short of their best. We should shoot for the best, and if at the end of it all, we end up being equal, we can live with it. But it would be sad to stop at equal, when we could be so much more.

It also places our children at a disadvantage to strive to be equals with people who believe they are better. Lastly, equality locks in the mind at the level of the person or group that you believe is your equal. If I only thought myself equal to my opponent, and he ran a 4.3 second 40 yard dash, I would never had broken 4.2 because I would have only envisioned 4.3 because I saw myself as equal. You must feel that you are greater in order to achieve greater things. There is no dishonor or arrogance in believing in your greatness. I would rather be considered arrogant and excel than to be considered humble and fail.

Not everyone will believe in this frame of mind, and that is their prerogative. I will simply use sports analogies to make my point Many of the legends that we celebrate were considered arrogant, from Muhammad Ali to Richard Sherman, they are reviled because they openly declared that they were the greatest in their respective sports; however, their accomplishments make it hard to argue with them.

There is no calamity which a
great nation can invite which
equals that which follows a
supine submission to

wrong and injustice

and the consequent loss of
national self-respect and honor,
beneath which are shielded and
defended a people's safety and
greatness.

Eldridge Cleaver

Chapter 6

The Psychological Trauma of Slavery

Actually, when it comes to the struggle in the African American community, there are a number of elephants in the room, beginning with white supremacy racism; however, there is very little in the way of meaningful discussion when it comes to dealing with the issues that are inextricably connected to the psychological trauma associated with slavery. Before moving into this, I believe it is important to explain why the psychological trauma of slavery is so relevant to the problem of mis-educating our youth.

When you understand that the inculcation of erroneous information that is consistently forced into the informational gates of our youth are not simply building negative paradigms, but reinforcing existing paradigms that are diametrically opposed to the mindset that leads to authentic and complete black empowerment, you will be able to see why we must seize control of the process of educating our children. Honestly, no one wants to deal with the elephant in the room as far as the psychological trauma associated with slavery is concerned, including blacks.

It is obvious why whites don't want to deal with it. It makes them uncomfortable. Engaging the truth about slavery and the psychological damage that it caused creates a high level of cognitive dissonance for whites. You see, admitting that horrible atrocities were perpetrated against blacks on a systematic level is extremely hard to reconcile with the moral standard that white America attempts to push off on the rest of the world. Engaging the truth concerning the psychological wounds that blacks have carried all the way from slavery makes whites deal with those dirty little secrets that they want so badly to forget.

Admitting that slaves were terrorized in unimaginable ways also completely eliminates the argument that we need to just move on and let it go. Ignoring the issue allows the system to continue to wreak havoc on blacks as we continue to struggle with the psychological scars associated with slavery. Blacks don't really want to deal with it, because they don't want to make the whites in their periphery uncomfortable, which is actually a part of the mentality that is an integral part of this trauma. While everyone is pretending that nothing is wrong, the systematic reinforcement of the mindset created by slavery continues to render our people incapable of rising to the level of their design.

I am not one that believes in committing a great deal of effort to the task of convincing white people of the presence of racism, nor do believe that there is any benefit in getting them to admit that slavery traumatized blacks. Although I don't bar myself from discussion with whites on the issue, it is not my primary focus to get them to understand. Too much emphasis has been placed on controlling what the white man thinks, when it is what the black man thinks that will change our situation. So, it is in our best interest to admit that this issue exists, not for the sake of wallowing in the mire of its results, but for the sake of dealing with it and healing from it, so that we can move forward triumphantly.

There has been a significant amount of research and work done on the topic. Probably one of the most comprehensive and lucid expressions of this truth can be experienced through the work of Dr. Joy DeGruy, the author of *Post Traumatic Slave Syndrome: America's Legacy of Enduring Injury and Healing*. This book goes into substantial detail in uncovering the devastating effects that slavery had on blacks, but what I love most about this book is the fact that the primary objective is healing. One of the problems with blacks is that we tend to wallow in our negative situations. We spend far too much time pointing the finger at the problem and those who perpetrated these negative actions towards us, or those who are currently perpetrating these negative actions, instead of taking action. Dr. DeGruy focuses on healing; nonetheless, healing begins with acknowledging that there is an illness or injury from which healing must occur.

Although there is not enough time to really open up the depth of the psychological trauma associated with slavery, I do want to touch on some key points that are presented by Dr. DeGruy, and I want to close out the loop by tying the current education system to this trauma—showing how the mis-education of our youth serves to reinforce the negative self-images that we have as a group of people—images that are a direct result of slavery, which points back to my call to create more powerful and positive images for our youth.

I will use only one example from Dr. DeGruy's book to make my point on a broader scale. In her book she tells this story of two white men who work together in the same office for 20 years. They work on projects together. They golf together, and they attend company functions simultaneously, however, they both despise each other. They talk behind each other's back, and they attempt to undermine the reputation of the other. They even work to beat the other out of the next promotion opportunity. What is key about this relationship is that despite the fact that they cannot stand each other, they work together for the common cause of completing projects because that is how they collect their paycheck—allowing them to provide for their families.

DeGruy then points to the fact that certain cultural and psychological impediments would almost certainly create a situation in which this type of functionality would not be possible if it were two black men in the same situation. While the white men tacitly agreed not to openly acknowledge their animosity or their true feelings concerning the other, the two black men would find the same course of action to be next to impossible. This mindset by blacks is based on the fact that relationships play a preeminent role in African American culture, which makes it extremely difficult to overlook the fact that someone does not like you. Where it is of little consequence in white culture, it will likely lead to a confrontation, and maybe even a physical altercation when two black men are placed in that situation.[1]

It is the manner in which blacks view relationships that would create the impasse. In African American culture, relationships trump everything else. Although we often respond in ways that can be detrimental to our well-being when we feel we are not liked, our focus on the importance of relationships has also served to strengthen and galvanize us in the past, and we must find a way to get back to the point in which our focus on relationships serves us instead of dividing us and creating impasses.

The psychological impact of slavery can be seen in the way we treat our children—how we speak to them and even how we punish them. The dominative form of parenting that dares a child to ask questions or challenge a decision is not African in nature, it is a direct

---

[1] DeGruy, *Post Traumatic Slave Syndrome.*

result of slavery, an institution that did not allow slaves to challenge or question their masters. Limiting the ability of a child to question things will diminish their capacity to effectively function within the confines of critical thought. Black children who are not allowed to ask "why" will eventually develop a mindset that demands that there is always someone who is telling them what they need to do.

When consideration is given to the fact that the majority of these homes in which this is being practiced is headed by a woman, it gives even greater gravity to the issue at hand. Any black male child that is consistently dominated by a woman, even his mother, will develop a defeated and docile spirit when it comes to women. He will actually seek out women that will tell him what to do. This means that he has been completely incapacitated as far as his ability to lead is concerned. This form of emasculation is not by accident, as you will see later on in the book.

In essence, instead of educating and empowering our children to be independent thinkers, we passed on our personal inadequacies and diminished self-worth in the form of degradation and domination. How many times have you heard a black mother yell, "You ain't never going to be nothing (insert expletive); you are going to be just like your daddy." We speak into our children's lives every time that we engage them, and they hear us loud and clear. The opportunities that we have to empower them are squandered away because we can't get past our own sense of inadequacy. This is so important to understand when you consider the fact that almost all intellectual stimulation and imagery that our children will encounter in this world will portray them in a negative light. This means that it is imperative that we con-sistently impart a sense of value and purpose into their lives. We must inculcate their true identity into the deepest aspect of their psyche, so that when information that is contrary to the truth of their existence is presented, they will have the capacity to override it and immediately dismiss it.

To this point, we have only served to reinforce the negative imagery that they have been bombarded with, and then we send them to a public school that is designed to diminish them, expecting them to succeed. We must do a better job of protecting the self-image and self-worth of our children. We must guard it with all diligence. We must not allow our proclivity to trust everything white to force us to place our children in harm's way.

We must become the primary educators, and we must also be the ones that guard the gates of our children to ensure that nothing that has the capacity to harm them enters those gates. Yes, it is a challenge, but that is a challenge that we must be able to meet. It is foolish to trust something of such significance to those who actually benefit from our demise. We are simply too trusting, and it is costing us dearly.

As a race of people, we have proven that we have the resilience to survive the most pernicious of attacks over and over again, so we know that we are capable of healing from the psychological scars of slavery. Healing is vital to the complete elevation and empowerment of our people. While we fight to achieve healing, we must not be guilty of passing along the pain to our progeny. We must commit to ending the cycle of dysfunctionality, and we must focus on using the strength of our view of relationships to draw us together as a unified people. We have to have a certain level of self-love in order for this to work.

It has to be viewed as unacceptable to be assaultive toward another black, and this begins at home with our mate and our children. We must also come to an understanding that just because it was done to us, does not make it a good idea. As I counsel families, I hear often, "My mother did it to me, and I turned out fine." Well, actually, you didn't turn out fine, you are sitting here talking to me. And, even if a person was able to overcome certain hostile treatment as a child to become a productive and functional part of society, it does not make it a good idea to pass that hostility on to their child.

I am not here arguing for or against corporal punishment, but I believe that we all know when we have gone past what should be acceptable as punishment and entered into the realm of abuse. This is why having a lucid perspicacity of our history beyond slavery is so important. The type of corporal punishment that we unleash on our kids is not a part of our African heritage, it is a part of our heritage as descendants of slaves.

With this broken mindset, our children are already broken by the time they reach the public school system, making them extremely vulnerable to the machinations of that malicious system. We must guard the minds of our youth, and we must protect their spirit, until it has the time to develop to a level in which it can guard itself.

I've never seen a sincere white
man, not when it comes to
helping black people. Usually
things like this are done
by white people to benefit
themselves. The white man's
primary interest is not to
elevate the thinking of black
people, or to waken black
people, or white people either.
The white man is interested
in the black man only to the
extent that the black man is of
use to him. The white man's
interest is to make money, to

exploit.

Malcom X
Playboy Interview
1963

Chapter 7

False Liberation: The Dangers of Illusion

As stated earlier, it is important to view education in its proper context. When I speak of education, I am speaking of the holistic process through which our youth are indoctrinated and prepared for the life ahead of them. This type of educational process transcends a solitary academic program. Although academics are a significant aspect of the educational process, they are far from constituting its totality. In fact, there are many instances in which academics are over emphasized. Too much gravity is given to academics, with very little emphasis being placed on the aspect of individual personal development and critical thought.

It is not my intent to marginalize the importance of academic disciplines; they definitely have their place in the educational process. However, human development is an individual process that must be engaged with a certain level of specificity, requiring that a child's individual gifts and passions are nurtured and empowered. Standardized academic programs serve to stifle the progressive development of children. Due to the fact that the current public education system is one of European descent—designed to serve the Eurocentric focus of this country—it serves to stifle the growth and productivity of black children at an alarmingly disproportionate rate.

You may be asking yourself, what does the illusion of liberation have to do with the mis-education of black youth? If you have not yet reconciled your thinking to line up with the holistic concept of education, it will be difficult for you to see the correlation, but I will do the best that I can to erase the nebulosity that may be present.

The educational process is extremely comprehensive, involving all conduits and mediums that are used to disseminate information to the individual who is being educated. This means that the illusion of liberation, which serves as a distraction to blacks—a major diversion from the reality in which we truly live—is reinforced through the educational process. This leaves our children embracing the same false reality that has served to keep us stagnant for the last 50 years. The illusion of liberation and progression will keep our people fighting to progress using the same methods that we have always used. It will continue to distract us from the critical thought and progressive planning necessary to build our own economic system, as well as restore our family nucleus.

In essence, our children are being conditioned to perpetuate the nothingness that has been perpetuated by blacks for 150 years—yet we have actually made no progress. If we continue to allow our children to be systematically fed these illusions, we will find ourselves on the edge of extinction within the next two decades.

THE BLACK RACE IS IN TROUBLE

Since slaves were quasi-freed in 1865, there has been a consistent assault against the black race, with a focus on keeping us distracted while we are being systematically destroyed. There has been a consistent illusion of progression presented for the purpose of convincing the masses that we are gaining ground. This produces a fervor to press forward using the same focus and methodology that we have always used. The problem is that the progression that we believe we have achieved is an illusion, subsequently rendering all of our current efforts useless.

The success of black business moguls, such as Oprah and Tyler Perry, or athletes, such as LeBron James and Kobe Bryant, present an illusion that blacks are progressing. However, when you examine this illusion on a platform that actually matters, the ownership of wealth, you can gain a more lucid understanding of just where we are as a race of people.

On the eve of the civil war, there were approximately 300, 000 quasi-free blacks, and they had managed to amass one-half of one percent of the total wealth of this nation. Here we are 150 years later, and we still own only one-half of one percent of our nation's wealth. What this means is that although there has been some individual progress, such as can be observed with black professional athletes, the total disparity between blacks and whites, especially in the area of economics, has remained consistent since slaves were freed.

The success of a few is used to create the image of progression, diverting attention from the fact that no true progress has been made. This illusion was definitely magnified with the election of Barack Obama to the White House

Dr. Claud Anderson explains this quite lucidly in his book, *Black Labor, White Wealth*. He writes that shortly before the Civil War:

> Records indicated that more than 50 percent of free blacks were paupers; all free blacks collectively held less than one half of one percent of the nation's wealth . . . A century later, in the 1960s, an era considered by many as the 'great decade for blacks,' more than 55 percent of all the blacks in America were still impoverished and below the poverty

line. And, blacks barely held one percent of the nation's wealth.[1]

What is even sadder is the fact that we are now in a worse position than we were in the 1960s. When inflation is considered, and all economic variables are considered, blacks remain the most impoverished race in America, with only microcosmic growth being experienced over the last 50 years. Even those whom we view as being successful, depend on a white financial system to supply their income, meaning that although they are being enriched, their gifts and talents are being used to enrich their white benefactors at a much greater rate.

The truth is that equality is not obtained through social acceptance, integrated matriculation, or any form of integration, for that matter. The only way that true equality can be measured is in the presence of equal opportunity, and in a capitalist system, opportunity is created through ownership and control. As long as blacks fail to acquire ownership and control, there will be no true equality. However, the masses have been distracted by the illusion of progress, and many blacks find themselves living vicariously through those whom they perceive to be successful. Collectively, we have failed to see the writing on the wall. The game is being played out on the grand chessboard of life, and we have allowed ourselves to be placed in check, with very few moves for us to make that can free us from check and avoid a final checkmate.

We are at a critical point in which black group economics practiced vertically has to be the central focus. This is not only for the black adult population, but this mindset must be a part of the educational process for empowering our youth. They must have a mindset

[1] Anderson, *Black Labor, White Wealth.*

of ownership and control in order to effectively use the academic aspect of their education to carry out the responsibility of acquiring true wealth through ownership and control.

We must begin to teach our youth in the same manner that the wealthy teach their children. The focus has to shift from getting an academic education so that they can get a job with a Fortune 500 company to expanding their education for the purpose of building wealth as they build their own Fortune 500 companies that will rival the companies of their white counterparts.

WORKING THIS THING OUT

We are under assault. Whether it is mass incarceration, the abortion epidemic, chronic poverty, or a number of other mechanisms perpetuated against us by white supremacy, we are being constantly bombarded by machinations that are designed to destroy us, or at the very least, marginalize us. We have spent too much time focusing on the wrong thing. This means that we must make a decisive move to correct our direction. As blacks, we must create our own black economic infrastructure that is designed to redirect the focus of the black dollar, so that we can start investing in black businesses in a manner that will allow us to dominate every industry in which we dominate the spending.

There is no way that we should completely dominate the spending in any industry and not dominate business ownership in that industry as well. The beauty supply industry is a $15 billion a year industry, and 96 percent of that annual revenue is generated by blacks, meaning that more than $14 billion dollars of this industry comes from the pockets of blacks. However, blacks only own three percent of the businesses in the industry. This has to change. We must be willing to engage in building vertical enterprise in this industry, meaning that we must own businesses at every level—retail, distribution and manufacturing, etc. That is how you dominate a market and industry. This way, no external entity can price you out of business.

While the adults are laying the foundation for this, we must be teaching our children this practice and mindset from an early age, so that it is instilled into their psyche. This is how we break the chains of bondage that still hold us back; not by begging for relief or appealing to the sympathy of those who oppress us. Freedom is something to be seized not negotiated.

All peoples are struggling to
blast a way through the industrial
monopoly of races and nations,
but the Negro as a whole
has failed to grasp its true
significance and seems to delight
in filling only that place
created for him
by the white man.

Marcus Garvey
Opinions and Philosophies
of Marcus Garvey
1923

Chapter 8

Erroneous Expectations

I have to admit that there are a lot of things that frustrate me concerning the current state of Black America; however, there are very few things that frustrate me more than the collective yearning of blacks to be accepted, protected and liberated by white America. This almost natural yearning to be accepted by white America is one of the most crippling mindsets that we, as a people, can have. The thought process behind this way of thinking is dangerous in a number of ways. First of all, as long as we are looking to white America for liberation and acceptance, we will never become accountable for our own actions, subsequently leaving us powerless to exact change on our own.

One would be hard pressed to find a black leader that emphasized the importance of struggle in the process of seeking freedom more than Frederick Douglass. In his 1857 speech, "If There is No Struggle, There is No Progress," Douglass makes it lucidly clear that liberty and freedom must be demanded from the oppressor in action, not just words:

> The general sentiment of mankind is that a man who will not fight for himself, when he has the means of doing so, is not worth being fought for by others, and this sentiment is just . . . Such a man, the world says, may lie down until he has sense enough to stand up . . . Let me give you a word of the philosophy of reform. The whole history of the progress of human liberty shows that all concessions

yet made to her august claims have been born of earnest struggle. If there is no struggle, there is no progress. Those who profess to favor freedom and yet depreciate agitation are men who want crops without plowing up the ground; they want rain without thunder and lightning. They want the ocean without the awful roar of its many waters.[1]

No race or nation has ever won its freedom from its oppressor by appealing to their sympathy or moral turpitude. The fact that this nation kept us enslaved for 300 years reveals the evil intent that it had for blacks. We were never meant to be included in the promises to have access to the pursuit of happiness. We were brought to this nation for the sake of being the working class, and the intention was to obtain free labor.

We must be willing to accept the fact that slaves were not freed due to some moral epiphany, although many have attempted to sell that myth. The truth is that freeing the slaves was expedient to the objective of saving the union. The economic advantage that slave ownership gave the South over the North could not continue and the Union remain actively functional. We cannot expect any group of people who benefits from our oppressed state to actively play a role in our liberation.

ECONOMIC EMPOWERMENT

The elevation of the black race begins with black group economics—practiced vertically. This is not the only time that you will see this statement made in this book, because it is the most vital element of black elevation. Group economics serves a multiplicity of purposes. First of all, it provides the autonomy necessary for blacks

[1] Frederick Douglass, "If There is No Struggle, There is No Progress," 1857.

to rise up from our current state of oppression. It creates the foundation to support every strategic plan necessary to build up the black community.

As more and more blacks in America become cognizant of the true culprit associated with their perpetual struggle, they are left with the problem of deciphering the codes that will allow them to break free of the chains of bondage that effectively limit them in their quest for empowerment. To gain a lucid understanding of the primary issue that underwrites the suffering of blacks, one only needs to examine the aggregate economic prowess of blacks in America. Because of the lack of practicing black group economics, white supremacy racism has made easy work of keeping blacks in a position of economic futility and impotence.

ECONOMIC CASTRATION

From the beginning, blacks in America, as a whole, have been kept out of the fluid flow of the economic infrastructure in this country. When the Civil War ended, blacks in this country had managed to gain ownership of one-half of one percent of this nation's wealth. Here we stand 150 years later, and blacks still own only one-half of one percent of this nation's wealth. In order for that to happen, there has to be a deliberate system in place that ensures it.

In order for blacks to compete in the national economy, they must have equal footing in the game. Dr. Claud Anderson makes this analogous to the game of Monopoly. We have all played the game at some point in our lives. The key to the game is that everyone starts out with the same amount of money. As the game progresses, the participants acquire land, rental properties and businesses. The one who is best at this wins. Now imagine having to start the game off with no money.

That is the burden that blacks have been shouldering for more than 150 years.

This is why the entire bootstrap concept has failed immensely for blacks. The rise of the talented tenth has presented a fallacious concept that offers the argument that all blacks have to do is pull up their boot straps and get to work. Just as Dr. Anderson has stated numerous times, blacks in America are trapped in a real live Monopoly game in which we own no wealth while attempting to compete with those who own the wealth. The deck is stacked.

BLACK EMPOWERMENT THROUGH GROUP ECONOMICS PRACTICED VERTICALLY

I have presented this truth on multitudinous occasions, and I will continue to push it until it finally registers in the mind of the majority of blacks in this country. We reside in a country in which the economy flows through the conduit of wealth. Without ownership of land, real estate properties, businesses and other wealth building assets, blacks will never be able to compete.

What we must understand is that the American government will never give us that fair footing that comes with ownership. This means that we must be willing to take it. How do we accomplish this? We take it through the practice of vertical group economics.

Allow me to elucidate the phrase, "vertical group economics." When I say that we should practice vertical group economics, most people envision blacks supporting only black owned businesses, and this is definitely a part of black group economics. Nevertheless, vertical group economics consists of much more than patronizing black businesses. Vertical group economics is the practice of group economics in a manner in which we seek to dominate an entire industry. For example, as stated in an earlier chapter, blacks generate 96 percent of the revenue in the beauty supply industry, but we only own three percent of the businesses in the industry at any level. We should completely dominate the industry.

To dominate the industry would call for ownership at every level, creating a vertical economic structure that would present the black retailer, who would purchase all of their supplies from the black distributor, who purchases their goods from the black manufacturer. All of this would begin with black designers, inventors and creators. In this system, there would be no need for black business owners to move horizontally out of their vertical economic infrastructure to do business with a non-black. As things stand now, even black business owners have to take black dollars to the economic structures of other groups in order to supply their businesses.

It is simple, if we want to build a powerful foundation, we must do it through black group economics practiced vertically.

We can see the fallacy in the education system all we want, but without the economic power to make changes, we are simply grasping at straws. With economic power, we can directly influence the methods through which our children are educated. We can also use this power to effectively influence the political processes that affect our children. Additionally, we will have the capital to invest in our children in a manner that allows us to facilitate the transition of their dreams into reality.

Black group economics opens the door to engage in the political process in a manner that will serve our interests and specific agendas. It will immediately provide the black community with a voice that it has lacked for decades. Blacks have bought into the myth that it is who you elect that matters; however, the Asian community completely dispels that myth. Asians, traditionally do not vote, but they have the highest earning median in the nation. This is because they invest a significant amount of money into the political process. They understand that it is not who you elect as much as who you fund.

Blacks must be willing to borrow a page from the books of other ethnic groups who have come to America and surpassed us. All other groups who come to America come to America viewing black communities as the foundation on which they will build their wealth. They depend on the lack of cohesiveness and universal support of black businesses. It was the Jews who entered into the black community first to build their wealth. While we were fighting for integration and the right to spend our money in white businesses, the Jews were buying up the businesses that we were abandoning to pursue integration. It seems that we failed to apprehend the fact that with the right to spend money in other economies other than our own, also came the natural decline of black ownership. We, in essence, began the process of financing our own demise as we poured our money into the white economy, while draining the life out of our own.

Another important result of black group economics is the sense of identity and accomplishment that it builds. Practicing black group economics presents the fact that we don't need to be dependent upon any other group or race. The mindset that fosters the belief that blacks need help from whites to liberate ourselves is deeply rooted in a perpetual inferiority complex. It is the belief that any group, other than ourselves, has more power to free us and offer us equal opportunity that handicaps black progression and empowerment.

LOWERING THE CRIME RATE AND INCARCERATION IN BLACK AMERICA

It is no secret that an increase in the level of poverty in any area will be followed by an increase in crime, regardless of race. So, there should be no surprise that the crime rates are high in our inner-city communities, when a significant number of our people are living at or below the poverty level. Creating our own economic infrastructure creates the opportunity to hire from within our community. It also presents a visual model of black success within the confines of the law.

This also means that we will be in a better position to provide jobs and programs for our men and women who are reentering society after serving time in prison. Black men are the most unemployed and underemployed group in the U.S., and this has a direct impact on the state of the black family and the black community. We will discuss this more in the next chapter.

We have to build our own, so that we can work to reduce the unemployment rate in our community, especially when it comes to our men. It is also vital that we reshape and represent the image of black men, and the black community as a whole. White supremacy has gone to great lengths to present an unflattering image of blacks that is not indicative of our race as a whole, and we must work diligently to reshape the image that is presented This is why ownership is so important. We cannot disseminate information through media channels that we do not own without the approval of those who own those channels. Subsequently, when the ones who own these channels are the very ones who are responsible for our current state and their success and ability to sustain their position is dependent upon our oppression, the chances are not good that they will offer us the help that we seek. We need to do as Tom Burrell said, use the system that is already in place to reverse the tide—implement positive propaganda to contrast the negative propaganda that the mainstream media is disseminating.[2]

---

[2] Tom Burrell, *Brainwashed: Challenging the Myth of Black Inferiority.*

We must relinquish the expectations that whites will ever have a moral epiphany, and subsequently decide to lift their foot off of our necks. The goal of whites, in general, is the same as it is for any other race of people—to survive—and to survive at the highest level possible. This means that not even your white friends are going to be willing to renounce their white privilege to ensure that you have a leg up in the world. Additionally, white supremacy America, which is representative of the wealthy elite that create geopolitical policies on a global scale that are designed to ensure that they maintain their stronghold, has absolutely no motivation to ease the oppression of blacks on a global scale. Actually, the fact that the blacks in America represent the wealthiest group of blacks on the planet has placed a target on our back, serving to intensify the efforts to destroy, or at the very least, neutralize us.

We must stop asking white America for their acceptance. We must also stop asking and demanding that they share their things with us. Instead of asking to be included in what they have, we must learn how to build and own our own. I read the other day where a brother stated that one of the reasons that whites are so hostile towards blacks is the fact that we are the only group that keeps demanding that they share their stuff with us, instead of building our own. That statement is highly profound. We spend far too much effort attempting to get white America to give us a piece of their pie, instead of baking our own. We must change that mentality.

DESTROYING THE MYTH OF BLACK ON BLACK CRIME

Another area of concern for me is this myth of black on black crime, and the manner in which it has impacted the lives of blacks. This myth places a disproportionate impression of violence on blacks, especially black men. This intentional machination of white suprem-acy is to present a negative image of blacks that drives fear. When people are afraid, they are less likely to protest the methodology that is used to remove the cause of their fear. This means that whites and others in America are less likely to become involved in standing up against the wrongful murders of black men by white cops, because the nucleus of their greatest fear is inextricably bound to the black man.

More importantly, when young black youth consistently see this image, they begin to believe the negative story about themselves, and what a person believes has a massive impact on their behavior and their aspirations. It also provides a built-in excuse for erroneous be-havior. When a child believes that they are predisposed to violence, it makes it easier for them to justify violent behavior.

The pernicious effects of this myth run even deeper. The por-trayal of black on black violence as some sort of social anomaly serves to lay the foundation for the marginalization of black life. It sends a message that because these people kill each other without pause, they cannot possibly have a high value on life. It is this mindset that makes it easy to pull a trigger and take a life, because the message has already been sent that black lives are of little to no value.

What is key here is that we should not be looking to white Amer-ica or the government to deal with this problem for us. This is some-thing that we should be dealing with ourselves. We owe it to our youth to educate them in a way that they see value in their existence, individually and collectively. It is time that we rewrite our story. It is time that we take on a pride that drives us to tell our story our way. We have come to a point in which this natural proclivity of ours to seek the approbation of others must be cast away. We must learn to celebrate who we are, where we have come from and the power to travel the road to our destiny—a destiny of greatness and autonomy.

The truth is that violence involving blacks against other blacks is not an anomaly. In fact, it is a cultural norm that is present in every ethnic group. Violent crimes are usually crimes of passion, and crimes of passion are usually perpetrated against those whom we know. According to statistics released by the FBI, white on white crime has reached epidemic proportions, with 83 percent of white murders being committed by a Caucasian assailant. When this is compared to the 90 percent rate of black murders committed by a black assailant, there is very little disparity, especially when consideration is given to the fact that blacks are living at a higher rate of poverty than whites. So, if you remove the poverty divide, the rate of same race crimes would be about equal.

This is no way means that there is not a problem with violence in the black community, it simply suggests that blacks are no more proclivitous to violence than any other racial group. Our current situation simply increases the instances of violence.

DESTROYING THE MYTH OF BLACK INFERIORITY

Tom Burrell goes to great lengths to reveal how mainstream media is used to present a message of inferiority when it comes to blacks. It is important to understand that a 400-year campaign has been launched to promote the superiority of the white race in the eyes of blacks. The counter-result of this campaign is a deep-seeded inferiority complex suffered by blacks collectively.

This myth of black inferiority was initially created as a way to justify slavery in a democracy. It has continued as the method used to subdue and subjugate blacks. The primary methods of disseminating this myth is through mainstream media. It is mainstream media that is primarily responsible for pushing the message of black inferiority. In fact, mainstream media should be viewed as the messenger that is promoting one of the greatest lies in American history—black inferiority. Through this comprehensive campaign, blacks have adopted a number of habits that have proved extremely detrimental to us. One habit that has proved to be highly detrimental is consumerism. Because blacks have never had status in this country, and we are so desperate to escape the valley of perceived inferiority, we attempt to buy our way out.

A significant amount of the money that we spend as consumers is spent on status items, including cars, clothes and jewelry. There are two problems that are created by this mindset. The first is the fact that we are spending more than we make on items that we believe will cause our oppressors to accept us. We have not yet learned that our value is within us. Our value is in our creativity and spirituality. You cannot examine any of the arts and not see our impact. Unfortunately, we have allowed others to rob and pilfer our creativity, but that does not change the fact that we are exceptionally creative and innovative.

The second problem is that any time a group of people function solely as consumers, meaning that everything that they buy is manufactured and produced by someone else, they will always find themselves at the bottom of the socioeconomic ladder. In order to understand the current plight of blacks, and to dispel the myth of black inferiority, it is vital to gain an apprehension of the unique context through which blacks entered this county. We are completely unique in this way. Every other group came to this country of their own free will, and they were supported as they proceeded to build their lives.

On the other hand, we were brought here against our will, under substandard conditions, and we were given no rights. The words of Supreme Court Justice, Roger Taney, still ring out: "The black man has no rights which the white man is bound to respect."

We have spent our entire existence here in this country attempting to find ourselves. We have spent a gargantuan amount of energy attempting to convince others, including ourselves, that we are worthy of their presence. That alone proves that we are struggling with our identity and self-image. It will take a great deal of effort to expose one of the greatest lies that has ever been perpetuated in this country—black inferiority. It starts with giving our youth adequate exposure to their complete history, not just slavery. We must connect with our heritage of royalty and greatness.

The educational system of a country is

WORTHLESS

unless it [revolutionizes the social order]. Men of scholarship, and prophetic insight, must show us the right way and lead us into light which is shining brighter and brighter.

Carter G. Woodson
The Mis-education
of the Negro
1933

Chapter 9

The Role of Black Men

I am the product of an inner-city community, and what I can tell you is that the entire filial dynamic in that neighborhood today is completely different than it was when I was growing up there.

First, the male presence in the community has diminished, and this means that the dominate masculine energy that is designed to guide young boys as they discover themselves and set out on life's journey is absent—leaving young boys to engage life from the perspective of their mothers and the guidance of the streets—an extremely dangerous combination. Even those who escape, lack the masculinity to lead our people. They achieve a semblance of success, but it is an illusion associated with assimilating into a system that is antithetical to black progress.

When we evaluate the machinations of white supremacy, we must do so at a molecular level. Blacks have a tendency to view every incident as an individual occurrence, instead of seeing it as being systemic. When we study the mechanisms of white supremacy racism, we have more than sufficient empirical and pragmatic evidence that their system is effective. This does not mean that the system is impenetrable, it simply means that its impact is real, and it must be dealt with decisively. This means going beyond simply talking about it.

The problem that we are facing now is that we have two primary sides of the equation that have been oversimplified. One side speaks of gentrification, mis-education, negative propaganda, and all of the other pernicious machinations of white supremacy as if they have been levied on blacks by God himself—taking on a defeatist mindset that there is no hope. On the other side of the spectrum, there are those of us that use our personal experiences to suggest that white supremacy is just an illusion, and that its power is only a figment of our imagination.

Here is the problem: Those of us who have escaped the grasp of the manacles of white supremacy racism, at some level, must come to understand that we are a part of an anomaly that can be identified by a number of monikers, including the "Best and Brightest" or the "Talented Tenth." Unfortunately, the vast majority of us take either of three positions—none of which are conducive to the elevation and empowerment of the collective.

1. Those who believe all blacks have to do is simply pull themselves up by their bootstraps.

2. Those who spend an exorbitant amount of time attempting to convince everyone, including themselves that there is nothing special about them. The "I'm just an average black man" complex.

3. Those who are only concerned with themselves, completely missing the fact that their existence is inextricably bound to the plight of all blacks.

I am a firm believer that white supremacy absolutely has no power that is not afforded to it through black compliance. We give every last one of their machinations power in our lives and community by accepting them as sovereign.

With that being said, here is the challenge. Just because we made it out, we cannot believe that all will have the fortitude and guidance that we had. That would be ignoring the current state of the black inner-city neighborhoods. We must be willing to accept the fact that we are different and that comes with a prodigious responsibility to reach back into the community in order to interpolate our wisdom, strategies and leadership.

We must be willing to understand that decisions are always limited to the choices one believes they have. It is our responsibility to expand the choices that our young men and women in the inner city currently have. This will call for a paradigm shift.

Make no mistake about it, the diminishing presence of the black man in the black community is by design. That alone causes me to have a healthy respect for my enemy, but it is that same fact that drives me to dethrone them. Anything that can be done can also be undone. The key is that we need our MEN to step up and step out into our communities.

If we want to make a difference, we must be present in our communities.

This can be a truth that is difficult to understand, being that we are the only group in America that functions under a matriarchy. We are the only race or social group in America in which there is a social organization through which relationship and descent are reckoned through the female line, and I would argue that it is no coincidence that we are the only group that is completely powerless to control our own destiny. Historically, the marginalization of the male role is always followed by a decline in social, financial and moral status.

This is definitely not an attempt to minimize the role of black women, I cherish them far too much for that; however, it is imperative that the balance in the black community is restored. It is absolutely vital that the roles of the black man and woman are cogently defined. Living in a social culture in which the woman is glorified and the man minimalized has not come without consequence.

Historically, the role of the man, husband and father has been held in high regard, but in this western culture, the role of the man has been relegated to filling space in the home and dropping off his paycheck. It is the woman who makes all of the decisions, under the guise of "women know best." It is the woman who draws the greatest reverence from their children. If you need a simplified microcosm that is representative of this fact, look at the way that Mother's Day is viewed and engaged juxtaposed to that of Father's Day. Even in school growing up, you could get away with saying something negative about a child's father, but the same words directed at their mother would almost certainly be met with a violent response.

There is nothing wrong with defending the honor of your mother, but there is a problem with not having equal reverence for your father. After all, it is the father who is the bearer of the identity of his progeny. It is the father who establishes the sense of self-worth for his children, especially his daughter. Historically, it was the father who named the child. From a historical perspective, a name has always been essential to the identity of the child. It was a major part of establishing their identity and purpose. When fathers named their children, it was a way of speaking into their lives and setting their paths. Unfortunately, today, a child is lucky if they end up with their father's last name.

Don't get me wrong, I am completely cognizant of the fact that black men share in the culpability associated with our current situation. I understand that we have collectively failed to walk in our divine purpose. This is not a finger-pointing session. There is a great deal of tension between the black man and the black woman, and I will deal with that in the next chapter; however, we must find a way to get around our existing issues, while creating a paradigmatic shift in our thinking as it pertains to the roles that we play.

UNDERSTANDING THE ROLE OF THE BLACK MAN IN TODAY'S SOCIETY

The presence of the black man in the black community is vital, and the importance of the role he must play cannot be overstated.

Because we tend to see things superficially, the election of Barack Obama to the office of President of the United States helped to conceal the impotency of the black man as we currently stand. There is a general impression that the black man has arrived, but the truth is that black men have very little influence in this country or in our own communities. The fact that the black race is a matriarchy reveals that the power structure of the black community is actually controlled by the black woman. The vast majority of the spending decisions in black America are made by black women, and we know, through experiential observation, whoever controls the spending is in command of the power.

The problem with this is that white supremacy is designed around the oppression of the black man, because the creators of this system understood that a group of people will only be as strong as their male leadership. So, from the beginning, the plan has been to marginalize the impact of the black man at all cost.

Listen, many of you will not receive this well, but the election of Barack Obama was only the culmination of the "selection" of Barack Obama, and it was more of an accomplishment for the white elitist who selected him and fast tracked him to the White House to facilitate their agenda. The election of a black president may serve to provide a certain level of hope for the black community, but hope will never see fulfillment if we fail to see the truth, and to meet that truth with corrective action.

Barack Obama's presidency does not, in any way, diminish the oppressive conditions under which the black man currently exists, nor does it alleviate the monumental challenges that he faces daily.[1] It is imperative that we take the necessary steps to restore the black man to a position of importance in his family and in his community. This is especially true when it comes to how he is viewed as a husband and a father.

Yes, we have had some black men in powerful positions, but we have yet to see the correlation of these powerful assignments with the advancement of black men collectively. If anything, these appointments and elections have only served to create a nebulous environment that sends an ambiguous message concerning the state of black affairs. While there are great stories to be told about the accomplishments of black men, we must be willing to tell the stories of the masses. For every successful black man, there are hundreds or even thousands that are falling victim to a pernicious system that was devised for the purpose of destroying them, or at least, neutralizing their effectiveness.

We reside in a current state where more than a third of our children live in a severe state of poverty. Many live in an environment in which they do not know where their next meal will come from. They lack the confidence to write their own story. This is because they don't know who they are. They know their name, but they don't have a clue of how their name is connected to their destiny. Additionally, the great divide between the mother they live with and the father

---

[1] Nathan Hare and Julia Hare, "The Role of the Black Man in Today's Society," *The Black Man's Think Tank.*

that they long for is so vast that communication between the two is virtually non-existent.

The manner in which the mother refers to the father has created even greater ambiguity concerning the father, because the child must now reconcile the mother's assessment of the father with their incessant yearning to have him around. What is ironic is the fact that the contempt that the black woman has for the black man is inextricably bound to the fact that she has not yet reconciled herself to the truth that she needs him. You see, feminism and the western culture in which she lives has convinced her that she does not need a man. It has convinced her that her degree, her six-figure income and her $500,000 home has somehow released her from the greatest purpose of her design—to walk in harmony with a man for the purpose of carrying out a collective vision that has been merged into one cohesive thought.

Until the black man has resumed the role of leader, provider, protector, bearer of identity and the giver of self-worth, we will continue to struggle as a group of people who don't know who we are or where we are headed. The abstruseness of the current plight of the black man leaves much work to be done; however, it must begin with the black man being determined to live up to the level of his design. He must not be willing to accept a role of diminished capacity. He must know his worth and his purpose. This is vital, because he cannot successfully establish the identity of his children if he does not yet know who he is.

When it comes to the educational process, the ability of the black man to fulfill his role is vital. If we want our children to become intimately acquainted with the massive force associated with the power that is inherent within them, they must be able to see it modeled in their progenitor. The black man is the model of power and confidence for his people. If we don't present that image, it doesn't matter how much ground our women gain, we will be viewed as weak.

It is also important for the black man to reverse the roles that have been successfully shifted through a number of mechanisms within the white supremacy system. The shift I am speaking of is the shift in the roles of black men and women. There used to be a time in which driving through a black neighborhood would produce an image of working men and pretty women, but that image has been reversed. Riding through the black neighborhood will now render an image in which the women are working and the men are pretty. We have lost our way. We as men find it an acceptable course of action to allow our women to be exposed instead of being covered. This is why we have been pilfered in every way possible.

During slavery, we were sold off from our families, and we were not allowed to protect our women, but this is no longer the case. It is time to stand up, step out and rise up. It is time for us to understand that the proper education of our children begins with us—the unrelenting black man.

THE LOVE OF A BLACK FATHER

I just wanted to take a brief moment to commend our black brothers who fight hard to love and protect their progeny. With the black family nucleus having taken a major blow over the last 40 years, this is not an easy task, and it does not come without its challenges.

I don't deny that there are some fathers who have found it to be the acceptable course of action to procreate, and then abandon their progeny; yet those numbers are far lower than mainstream media, and even some within our own ranks would have us believe.

Despite the myth, black men love hard, and there are very few things that can break a man like the pain of his children, or the inability to be a part of their lives. For those fathers who have found yourselves in situations that are not highly conducive to maintaining a positive and influential relationship with your children, but you somehow find a way, I commend you.

To the father who engages the enigmatic conundrum of finding a way to be present in your child's life while being in a different city or state, I celebrate you. Your struggle does not go unnoticed.

Lastly, to the father who wants nothing more than to be a part of his child's life, but finds himself battling a mother who is determined to use the child as leverage to settle an old score, I am standing with you.

Now, to you mothers who actually have an ex who is fighting to be a part of their child's life, but you have determined that because he hurt you, he will not get to be a part of that child's life—shame on you. You are the worst kind of selfish. There are things that only that father can impart upon that child, such as identity and self-worth, and you are robbing your child of that source of strength they will need in order to be all they were designed to be. The crazy thing is that many of you are aware of this because you have suffered from lack of your father's presence in your life.

There is a growing consensus among black women that black men have grown cold and aloof. Allow me to explain something to you. When you see a man that is not able to see his kid, because the mother has successfully hindered the process, the straight face that you see is actually that man's attempt to hide the pain. He has trained himself not to show the pain or the hurt, but deep inside he is broken.

When I am counseling men who are dealing with this issue, I

get the same thing almost every time. When they first walk in, they present the impression that they are straight up hard—no signs of weakness, but less than five minutes in, when the kids are mentioned, the tears begin to flow. I realize that I am one of a few people that will ever even see this, because the harsh world in which he lives requires that he man up as soon as he walks out of that door.

How dare you think that you have ownership over that child? That child does not belong to you, it belongs to its own destiny, and the father plays a major role in them taking the most advantageous path to their destiny. I don't care what you and that person went through, if that man wants to be there, you have no right to stop him.

Lastly, to the low-life scum, like Steve Harvey, who continue to bad mouth, degrade and perpetuate the image of black men for the sake of elevating yourself and improving your standing among your white audience, shame on you. I have no respect for you whatsoever. You have been given a powerful platform from which to elevate your people, but you have chosen to elevate yourself.

Our men need to be built up and held up, because it is on the backs of our kings that we will rise up to the pinnacle of power and liberation. Black men, I challenge you to be worthy of the title "King!" Black women, I challenge you to invest your energy in lifting him instead of breaking him. You have been used long enough for that.

We have so much work ahead of us, but the mission will be so much more laborious when there is no harmony between our women and men. Our children need and deserve parents who are willing to make the selfless sacrifice of leaving the past in the past.

The black family survived
centuries of slavery and
generations of Jim Crow,
but it has disintegrated in
the wake of the liberals'
expansion of the

WELFARE
STATE.

Thomas Sowell
Liberalism vs Blacks
2013

Chapter 10

Restoring
the Black Family Nucleus

For those who know me, it is no secret that I believe that the restoration of the black family nucleus is paramount to the true elevation of the black race in America. The black family, and its core values have been decimated by abandonment and betrayal. With such distance and animosity between the two principal elements of our greatness—our men and women—we are facing a dilemma. We must determine how we will move beyond living in the illusion of the lie.

WE HAVE BEEN BAMBOOZLED

When anatomizing the conundrum that blacks face in our fight to rise above our current state, we must first realize that we have been sold a corrupt and erroneous bill of goods. We have been consistently and systematically fed a corporate lie that is complex in nature. The multitudinous facets of this monumental lie are far too many to attempt to deal with in this short book; however, I will endeavor to illuminate one aspect that has caused more damage than any other.

I often speak of the need for blacks to establish an economic center through which we can practice black vertical group economics for the purpose of overall empowerment; yet it would be remiss to overlook the elephant in the room that has been ignored for decades— the disintegration of the black family nucleus. The black family has suffered due to a thirst to live inside of an illusion created by the lie I mentioned earlier.

OUR WOMEN MISLED AND REDIRECTED

I will address our women first, because although their contribution to the disintegration of the black family is significant, it is easily understood. Because of the power of mental conditioning, a significant amount of women who read this will not receive it. That is understandable. I simply ask you to consider what is written, then challenge yourself to prove it wrong beyond the acquiescence to your emotions. In other words, take the time to conduct the necessary research to establish that point you believe. It is my belief that the genuine journey for truth and the elevation will illuminate paths that you have never before trodden.

There are some of my brothers who would say that the feminist movement was the greatest distraction for the black woman. I will definitely not argue that the feminist movement caused great harm to the black family, but there is something much more subtle and sinister lurking in the undercurrent of our struggle. It is the illusion of the perfect man; the knight in shining armor. The six-figure brother who has it all together.

Over the last 40 years, the black male-female relationship has been romanticized. With authors, such as Carolyn Zane, Rochelle Alers and others, flooding the book shelves and digital libraries with novels that portray men that have no weaknesses, flaws nor baggage. There has been an illusion created that sets the standards and expectations of women. Without even realizing it, black women have developed unrealistic expectations that black men in America cannot possibly meet. Please understand that I am not suggesting that a black woman should be willing to accept a man who does not have a vision for his life and is not willing to fight to lift himself up to the level of his design, but I am saying that consideration has to be given to the entire dynamic of what it takes to develop a black man, especially in America. Again, this chapter is not meant to be comprehensive, nor is it designed to create a 100 percent lucid analysis of the problem. I want you to think. There is obviously a problem, and pointing the finger at the other person has not worked out well for us.

These awesome novels and movies that we see set our expectations. For women, it gives them their check list. But allow me to pose a rhetorical question. How many of you ladies have met a man who filled your checklist, but when you got with him, there were still issues? I can guarantee you that the vast majority of you have to admit that this is true. When I conducted the research for my book, "When Your House is Not a Home," the numbers that I unveiled concerning black relationships were absolutely staggering. We lead the nation in divorce percentage. We lead the nation in single parent household percentage. We have developed a syndrome in which successful black men are no longer looking to get married, and those who are have determined that it is best to marry outside of their race. We have problems.

Here is one of the problems. The romanticizing of the black male-female relationship has supplied our women with the wrong questions to put on their checklists. Instead of inquiring about his bank account, home, and career, the questions should be more vision oriented. Instead of asking a man where he works and lives, a woman should simply ask him what the vision that he has for his life is. Where he works and lives tells you where he is at, but his vision will bring illumination to where he is going.

This is important because the woman will play a significant role in this man's vision. This is another area in which women have been misled; they are looking to find men that have it all together when they meet them. The truth is that there will be certain things that the man will not achieve without the woman to incubate it and give it life. If you meet a man who does have it all together, be certain that you are entering into a situation in which another woman nurtured and brought his vision to life. Be careful. You need to do your own nurturing. You need to give birth to your own situation.

One of the problems facing black women now is that they don't want to endure the filling of their spiritual womb to birth the greatness in a man. They want a ready-made man like the ones they read about in books and see in movies.

Black women, it is your spiritual womb in which the seed of a man's vision is placed, incubated and birthed. You are the life source of his greatness. In the same way that his physical seed fertilizes the ovum in your natural womb and over 40 weeks returns to him his progeny, you must allow him to plant within your spiritual womb his vision and dreams. You must then incubate them and birth them—giving them spiritual life. He will know what to do with it from there. There is no bond more powerful than the spiritual bond created during this process.

OUR MEN ARE LOST, CONFUSED & FRUSTRATED

The problem with our men runs emphatically deeper. It finds its origin in the bed of slavery. Don't get me wrong, there are issues that black women have passed down through generations that have their seed of origin in the bed of slavery as well; still, I feel that we need to deal with one issue at a time.

White slave owners understood the strength of any group of people was their leadership—their men. We established this point in the last chapter. The men in any society offer providence, protection and leadership to their women and children. When you remove the man's power to lead, you can weaken the people and ultimately break him. This is done primarily by interfering with his primitive need to protect his woman and his progeny. That was the first thing that the white man did—ravage our women while we watched. They killed any of us who attempted to interfere.

After initiating the breaking process by raping our women, they returned our violated queens to our bed to finish the process of breaking us. How often would she remind him of his failure to protect her? How often would she tell him that he is not half the man that massa is?

Unfortunately, it did not stop there. After the incredible yearning of a man to protect his woman, comes the desire to nurture and protect his progeny. The white man used black men as breeding mechanisms, then to stop them from bonding with their progeny, they would sell them off to the next plantation owner for them to breed with other women. The black man learned to disengage from the connection to his progeny. He learned to see the black woman as the conduit of sexual pleasure, and little more. He learned to expect to have kids in multiple households by multiple women.

The psychological bonds associated with this behavior have created an environment in which far too many of our men have found it to be an acceptable course of action to procreate and then abandon our progeny, while even more think it to be acceptable to take a misogynistic approach in dealing with our women. No, I am not insinuating that most black men are trifling and sorry; that would be an erroneous assertion; conversely, I would assert—based on the exceptionally high divorce rate, and the number of single parent households, that we have collectively abdicated our roles as leaders, protectors and providers.

We have created some enigmatic and challenging situations for which we maintain responsibility. A significant amount of us have children in more than one household. We have bought into the lie that our only responsibility is a check every month and periodic visits. That is simply unacceptable. We owe our women and children so much more. It is our responsibility to be present in each home that we have fathered a child. For those of us who have fathered children in more than one home, this will be challenging, but we created the situation and we must own the responsibility that is associated with it. This extends beyond your financial responsibility to your child, and it absolutely includes the mother, especially if she does not have a husband covering her.

Men, the mother of your child became your family and your responsibility the moment you planted your seed in her womb. No matter how much she declares that she does not need you, regardless of how hostile she may be toward you, she is still your responsibility. So, you need to make your presence felt in that home. There is no excuse. If she won't allow you to come by, find a way to get them the things they need—her included. You are about to take a crash course in true responsibility, and the first thing that you are going to learn is that it is not about you. This is bigger than you and her. We must set the example for our kids, and our erroneous behavior is why generations after generations of blacks have made poor decisions in choosing a mate, and it is why we have failed in the area of owning our responsibility. We educate our youth through modeling more than we do with words. We have to develop a mindset that propels us into a different sphere of engagement as far as our men and women are concerned.

Ladies, this goes for you as well. He may be a jerk, but if he is putting forth the effort, don't marginalize his efforts. This sends the wrong message to the child. If he is strapped for cash, allow him to make his presence felt in other ways. Whether you understand this or not, the more you display that you have confidence in him, and the more support you offer, the more you will see him press to do better. It is in his DNA, he responds to your affirmations, not your assaults and insults. You have to understand that there is nothing stronger and more resilient on this planet than a black man. In fact, the only thing that has the power to break a black man is a black woman whom he loves. Following is a treatise that explains the contempt that our women have for our men and it also explains how our women have been used to emasculate our black men, and the impact that it is having.

CONTEMPT AND EMASCULATION AND HOW IT CONFUSES ROLES WITH OUR CHILDREN

Many of our men who have found themselves in a position of quasi-power have, in turn, allowed the mainstream media to emasculate them for the sake of a paycheck. Too many men have embraced fashion trends that display men in a feminine light. I hope that this part of this book will shake both men and women into a state of lucidity as far as the masculinity of black men is concerned.

Being a black man and having a clear understanding of my history, I am cognizant of the immense responsibility that I have to shed light on this controversial issue.

I will undoubtedly make some of you immensely uncomfortable while significantly aggravating and angering others. I understand that we live in a world in which most people don't want to stir the pot. We live in a world where everyone believes if it goes unspoken, then it doesn't exist. The problem is that this country is failing miserably and the failure lies at the feet of its men. It was the man to whom God gave the vision. It was the man that God gave dominion. It was the man that God entrusted to lead. When the man fails in his responsibility, everything in in his periphery suffers.

It is my intent to introduce black men to their greatest weakness and subsequently inspire them to walk in power. I also plan to introduce the black woman to her greatest weakness and how she is directly connected to the destruction and the emasculation of the black man. There are multitudinous queries into the current state of the black man. Why does he seem distant and aloof from his wife and family? Why does he have issues with being committed and honoring his marital responsibility? Why does he seem to have an innate proclivity to gravitate toward white women when he becomes successful?

To understand the dilemma of the black man in America, we must travel back to 1712. It was in 1712 that American slave owners were granted their wish by having Willie Lynch come to America to teach them how to control their slaves in a manner that would get the most productivity and profit out of them. Lynch was the owner of a plantation in the West Indies and he had gained notoriety for being able to manage his slaves. What you will find out as we examine what has become known as the "Willie Lynch Letter" is that when hanging, which eventually became known as lynching because of Lynch (who by the way, viewed hanging as waste of profit and productivity and a very last resort in mostly striking fear in recalcitrant black men) and whipping did not work in breaking the black man, they resorted to what they found was the only thing that could—his woman.

I will be sharing excerpts of the letter to give you a vivid picture of what has taken place over the last 300 years:

...I HAVE A FULL PROOF METHOD FOR CONTROLLING YOUR BLACK SLAVES. I guarantee every one of you that, if installed correctly, IT WILL CONTROL THE SLAVES FOR AT LEAST 300 HUNDREDS YEARS... I HAVE OUTLINED A NUMBER OF DIFFERENCES AMONG THE SLAVES; AND I TAKE THESE DIFFERENCES AND MAKE THEM BIGGER. I USE FEAR, DISTRUST AND ENVY FOR CONTROL PURPOSES. These methods have worked on my modest plantation in the West Indies and it will work throughout the South. Take this simple little list of differences and think about them. On top of my list is "AGE," but it's there only because it starts with an "a." The second is "COLOR" or shade. There is INTELLIGENCE, SIZE, SEX, SIZES OF PLANTATIONS, STATUS on plantations, ATTITUDE of owners, whether the slaves live in the valley, on a hill, East, West, North, South, have fine hair, coarse hair, or is tall or short. Now that you have a list of differences, I shall give you an outline of action, but before that, I shall assure you that DISTRUST IS STRONGER THAN TRUST AND ENVY STRONGER THAN ADULATION, RESPECT OR ADMIRATION.

The Black slaves after receiving this indoctrination shall carry on and will become self-refueling and self-generating for HUNDREDS of years, maybe THOUSANDS. Don't forget, you must pitch the OLD black male vs. the YOUNG black male, and the YOUNG black male against the OLD black male. You must use the DARK skin slaves vs. the LIGHT skin slaves, and the LIGHT skin slaves vs. the DARK skin slaves. You must

use the FEMALE vs. the MALE, and the MALE vs. the
FEMALE. You must also have white servants and overseers
[who] distrust all Blacks. But it is NECESSARY THAT
YOUR SLAVES TRUST AND DEPEND ON US.
THEY MUST LOVE, RESPECT AND TRUST ONLY
US. Gentlemen, these kits are your keys to control. Use
them. Have your wives and children use them, never miss
an opportunity. IF USED INTENSELY FOR ONE
YEAR, THE SLAVES THEMSELVES WILL REMAIN
PERPETUALLY DISTRUSTFUL.

Willie Lynch was a man that had studied the history of slavery
and the psychology of the slave. He had become a master at breaking slaves. He said that breaking a black male slave was analogous to
breaking a wild horse. The points in this that we are going to focus
on is the use of the black woman to break the black man, although it
will be important to pay attention to the impact it had on the kids as
a part of the educational and development process.

Historically, the black man was strong, not just physically, but mentally and spiritually. He did not break easily, but you are about to discover that the white man, discovered his vulnerability: the black woman.

Lynch taught the slave owners in Virginia that you break a slave
much in the same way that you break a horse. You must break them
from their natural state of existing. Remove the natural order. With
horses or humans, it is the natural order for the male to provide and
protect for the female and his offspring. Lynch's first principle was to
remove the ability for the man to provide or protect, so that he and his
family became dependent upon their white masters: but this was only
the beginning: ". . . we break that natural string of independence from
them and thereby create a dependency status, so that we may be able
to get from them useful production for our business and pleasure."

Lynch's plan ran much deeper than simply stripping the black man of his independence. Let's look at what else he suggested:

> Both horse and niggers [are] no good to the economy in the wild or natural state. Both must be BROKEN and TIED together for orderly production. For orderly future, special and particular attention must be paid to the FEMALE and the YOUNGEST offspring. Both must be CROSSBRED to produce a variety and division of labor. Both must be taught to respond to a peculiar new LANGUAGE. Psychological and physical instruction of CONTAINMENT must be created for both . . . NOTE: Neither principle alone will suffice for good economics. All principles must be employed for orderly good of the nation. Accordingly, both a wild horse and a wild or natural nigger is dangerous even if captured, for they will have the tendency to seek their customary freedom and, in doing so, might kill you in your sleep.

Everything that Lynch is presenting is built in first breaking the male. When the male is broken the world around him will collapse. What is interesting is that Lynch had discovered that hanging the black man did not break him. Hard work in the fields for long hours did not break him. Whipping him to within an inch of his life did not break him. Lynch had discovered that the only thing that could break a man was the contempt and disrespect of his woman. But how do you create an environment in which a woman would lose respect for her husband and treat him with contempt. Let's allow Willie Lynch to explain it in his own words. It is important to understand that it was not simply her contempt that broke him, but the reason for her contempt—his inability to function in his role. A man that can't protect and provide for his family will begin to question himself:

Hence, both the horse and the nigger must be broken; that is breaking them from one form of mental life to another. KEEP THE BODY, TAKE THE MIND! In other words, break the will to resist. Now the breaking process is the same for both the horse and the nigger, only slightly varying in degrees. But, as we said before, there is an art in long range economic planning. YOU MUST KEEP YOUR EYE AND THOUGHTS ON THE FEMALE and the OFFSPRING of the horse and the nigger. A brief discourse in offspring development will shed light on the key to sound economic principles. Pay little attention to the generation of original breaking, but CONCENTRATE ON FUTURE GENERATIONS. Therefore, if you break the FEMALE mother, she will BREAK the offspring in its early years of development; and when the offspring is old enough to work, she will deliver it up to you, for her normal female protective tendencies will have been lost in the original breaking process.

For example, take the case of the wild stud horse, a female horse and an already infant horse and compare the breaking process with two captured nigger males in their natural state, a pregnant nigger woman with her infant offspring. Take the stud horse, break him for limited containment. Completely break the female horse until she becomes very gentle, whereas you or anybody can ride her in her comfort. Breed the mare and the stud until you have the desired offspring. Then, you can turn the stud to freedom until you need him again. Train the female horse whereby she will eat out of your hand, and she will in turn train the infant horse to eat out of your hand, also.

When it comes to breaking the uncivilized nigger, use the same process, but vary the degree and step up the pressure, so as to do a complete reversal of the mind. Take

the meanest and most restless nigger, strip him of his
clothes in front of the remaining male niggers, the female,
and the nigger infant, tar and feather him, tie each leg
to a different horse faced in opposite directions, set him
afire and beat both horses to pull him apart in front of
the remaining niggers. The next step is to take a bullwhip
and beat the remaining nigger males to the point of death,
in front of the female and the infant. Don't kill him, but
PUT THE FEAR OF GOD IN HIM, for he can be
useful for future breeding.

Willie Lynch is getting to the heart of the matter. What is not
mentioned here clearly is exactly how he turned the woman against
the man? It is the man's responsibility to protect his woman. Taking a
black slave and raping her in front of her husband, showing her that
he had no power to help or save her, was all it took. Watching his
wife raped in front of him crippled him, but it was the contempt and
disrespect that he received from his wife daily that reminded him of
that helpless moment that broke him. Once the man was broken, he
was often bred for productive offspring and then sold off to break the
bond and ties to his family. The black male developed a proclivity to
move from plantation to plantation to father progeny that he never
stuck around to raise or care for.

Let's look at how Lynch then used the reverse effects that this had
on the women to break future black men while they were still boys:

By her being left alone, unprotected, with the MALE
IMAGE DESTROYED, the ordeal caused her to move
from her psychologically dependent state to a frozen,
independent state. In this frozen, psychological state
of independence, she will raise her MALE and female
offspring in reversed roles. For FEAR of the young male's
life, she will psychologically train him to be MENTALLY

WEAK and DEPENDENT, but PHYSICALLY
STRONG. Because she has become psychologically
independent, she will train her FEMALE offspring to be
psychologically independent. What have you got? You've
got the nigger WOMAN OUT FRONT AND THE
nigger MAN BEHIND AND SCARED.

Take a look at how this impacted the black marriage:

We breed two nigger males with two nigger females.
Then, we take the nigger male away from them and keep
them moving and working. Say one nigger female bears
a nigger female and the other bears a nigger male; both
nigger females—being without influence of the nigger
male image, frozen with an independent psychology—will
raise their offspring into reverse positions. The one with
the female offspring will teach her to be like herself,
independent and negotiable (we negotiate with her,
through her, by her, negotiates her at will). The one
with the nigger male offspring, she being frozen in
subconscious fear for his life, will raise him to be mentally
dependent and weak, but physically strong; in other words,
body over mind. Now, in a few years when these two
offspring become fertile for early reproduction, we will
mate and breed them and continue the cycle. That is good,
sound and long range comprehensive planning.

Okay, now let's take a real brief look at this point. It is simple, God
honors his men. He designed men to be honored. There is a certain
level of honor, even in discipline, yet the black man is one of the most
dishonored of men anywhere in the world. Who dares to dishonor
the black man? Contrary to popular beliefs and accusations, it is not
the white man.

Glance back to the beginning of this article and take notice of the word of Willie Lynch: "I HAVE A FULL PROOF METHOD FOR CONTROLLING YOUR BLACK SLAVES. I guarantee every one of you that, if installed correctly, IT WILL CONTROL THE SLAVES FOR AT LEAST 300 HUNDREDS YEARS."

It has been 303 years since Willie Lynch gave that speech. It looks like he underestimated the power of his system. Black women are still emasculating their men in both ways: disrespecting, dishonoring and being contemptuous toward their men and training their young boys to be psychologically weak and physically strong—perpetuating the cycle!

This is how the system has been perpetuated for centuries: While teaching her young male child to be weak, she is at the same time teaching her young female child to be psychologically independent and to treat all black men with the contempt associated with that independence: perpetuating the cycle of the broken black man.

In the natural order of things, a woman cannot be psychologically independent of the very thing for which she was designed and created. Through the combination of centuries of conditioning to break her man along with the contemporary cultural paradigms that convinces her she does not need a man, the woman has perpetuated the cycle.

Brothers stop blaming the white man, at least contemporary white men for breaking you and keeping you down. They don't have the power to do it. You are broken because your own support system is working against you. You must learn to stand up and function within your design and to guard yourself from the contemptuous woman who has become convinced that her strength is hidden in her power to break and handle you. You were designed to protect, provide and lead, but you can only accomplish this purpose with the one that recognizes and respects you as her leader.

You must also be willing to maintain a standard of masculinity. There is an old saying that states, "The clothes don't make the man, the man makes the clothes." Be the man that makes the clothes. Don't allow fashion designers to dictate what you wear. You have the capacity to sustain your dominion and power, but you must guard it at all cost. Remember, you are modeling what your offspring will become. You behavior is a part of the educational process of our youth. They are watching you.

Now, pay very close attention to what you are about to read, because this next statement is the most important of all. It is your responsibility to maintain and cultivate your manhood. Regardless of what has happened to this point, your manhood and masculinity is your responsibility. You can no longer blame the women, the system or your white counterparts. It is time for you, as a black man, to stand up and step out into your destiny. Yes, you have been under constant assault from the moment you were born, but the victim mentality does not wear well on you. You were born to be a king and a warrior. Our women need us to lead, even when they can't clearly see it. I would argue that despite the resistance, they want us to lead.

Sisters, I know that you have been hurt. I know that many of you have been disappointed. More than a small portion of you have suffered at the hands of a black man. Some black men have found it to be an acceptable course of action to procreate and then abandon you to raise their progeny on your own. Many have found it acceptable to step on your dreams and drain you of all hope. Many of you have been physically abused, the victims of incest and more. You have suffered and you have struggled. For every man that found it to be within reason to harm and hinder you, I personally apologize. You have been hurt, but you must understand that every word of contempt that you breathe toward a black man continues to diminish our race, and weaken our ability to establish a bright and prosperous future for our people.

No matter what secular culture is telling you, without the black man in a position of power to lead, our people will continue to wander astray. Granted, there are many men that are not ready to lead, but tearing them down will not prepare them to lead. Your true gift is in healing, encouraging and empowering. Trust me, he has enough people and situations telling him he is not good enough, smart enough and rich enough, and he does not need you to re-enforce it. If you can't say anything good. Simply hold your peace. Remember why you were created.

As a side note, the fact that I used the Willie Lynch Letter as the foundation for making my point here caught the attention of some, so I believe that it is fitting that I elucidate my position as far as this particular part of this book is concerned. There are a number of people who challenge the validity and authenticity of the Willie Lynch Letter. Many believe that it originated as late as 1970 and that Willie Lynch is a fictional character. It is not my desire to defend the authenticity of this letter, for whether or not the letter is authentic, the psychological principles are real. It is studied in institutions such as Howard and Harvard University. I first became aware of and studied the Willie Lynch Letter in college, and I pulled the quote from a copy taken from one of the most respected Universities in America. This does not authenticate the letter, but it does speak to its massive impact. It paints a real picture even if it is not real. Even a liar can tell the truth. Slavery broke down the black family nucleus. It robbed the black man of his power to provide for and protect his family. This would be true whether or not the Willie Lynch Letter ever existed.

The psychology of slavery is real and its effects are still prevalent today. To ignore them would only serve to extend the current level of bondage of our people. When coupled with the feminist movement, the psychology of slavery has literally strangled the life out of the black family by weakening its foundation—the black man.

We black men need women who will have our backs. We need women who we can trust with our weaknesses and vulnerability, without worrying about half of the world hearing about it.

One of my brothers in the struggle and I were watching old footage of the civil rights movement and we noticed something that totally blew our mind. When dogs and water hoses were turned on blacks, many women would get in front of their men almost instinctively. I decided to dig further to get an understanding of that phenomenon. What I found is that it is common for the women to sacrifice themselves for the man who was considered the future of the race or the people. This is even why the queen sacrifices herself for the king in the game of chess. Those women knew that if those men didn't survive to fight another day, their lives would completely change. Contemporary culture has convinced women that men were placed here for them when they have actually been designed for men.

This may sound crazy, but if you want your man to be the beast that he is designed to be, he needs to feel completely safe with you. You will never get all of him, if he does not trust you.

His heart rests with her, but if she shows him contempt and disrespect, it will drain him. It will cause him to withdraw in order to move back into a position of comfort and safety from the pain. Trust me, you don't want this, because it will be the child who pays for it the most.

In response to a question concerning the strength of a woman, I once wrote:

> They say that behind every good man is a good woman; I prefer to say that behind every great black man is a great black woman. Do you know why she is great? She is great because she knows his weaknesses, but instead of using them to degrade him or ridicule him, she comes along side of him, and as his missing rib, she covers his areas of vulnerability, allowing him to rise up and walk in his vision with the confidence of knowing that if he falls, she will still be there with him.

We need that great black woman to resume her role in the black community. We need black men to shake free of the egocentric mindset that has caused us to abdicate our throne. We need to cover our women with the magnanimous gift of unadulterated love. We need to shelter our children from the pernicious attacks of a system that is designed to devour their hopes and dreams.

My people, it is time to shake ourselves loose from the psychological bonds of slavery. It is time to exercise the demons of our past. No matter what you have been through, it is time to let it go and move forward. It is time to understand that this life is not about you; it is about you living in your purpose. It is time to usher in a brighter tomorrow for the next generation. It is time to rebuild the black family. This is about you living at the level of your design. It is about the unity and the elevation of a great and awesome people. We have been at the bottom too long. The time for change is now! This is why instilling absolute truth in our children is so important. We must take up the mantle and carry it to the finish line. Our children need us and the future of our race depends on it.

A LOVE THAT BREATHES LIFE

I was speaking with an immensely close friend of mine recently. Although we don't speak as often as we used to, I still love her dearly, as she has always been a good friend over the years. I also value her insight as a woman, as she embodies a lost art—although she is exceptionally intelligent and extremely independent, she is still a lady 100 percent through and through.

Last night we were discussing the conundrum of the black male-female relationship, and she said something so profound. She pointed to the fact that blacks who are in relationships actually trust their same-sex friends more than they trust their mates. In other words, there are things that they will share with their friends that they won't share with their mates. She iterated that this is from a lack of trust.

Here is where it got deep: She said that men no longer look to protect the heart of their women; even when they are good providers and they provide exceptional physical protection, they lack the understanding of the importance of protecting her heart and her emotional center.

Then I took it a step further, when I revealed that there is an equal force on the other side of this equation. Black women no longer understand the value of protecting and covering the weaknesses and vulnerabilities of their man. Too many women easily talk to their friends about their men's weaknesses, exposing him to ridicule.

When this dynamic is visited closely, it is easy to see why there is so much turmoil in black relationships, there is no trust; and where there is no trust, there is no cohesiveness.

Men, we have got to do a better job of protecting the hearts of our women, and ladies, you have to do a better job of covering the weaknesses and vulnerabilities of the black man. Without mutual trust, we are dead in the water.

Approximately one year ago, I had an epiphany that hit me like a ton of bricks. I was extremely frustrated with black women. Despite a strong yearning to settle down, and a fierce commitment to love a black woman only, I found myself on the verge of giving up on black women. However, there was a remnant of the true design that was present—a handful of women who understood their power, the importance of virtue and possessing an innate reverence for the man. That held me in check, and it would not allow me to give up.

While I was in a holding pattern, it hit me. It is up to the black man to love the black woman "back to life." In so many ways, she has been murdered, emotionally, psychologically and even spiritually, but instead of attacking her and degrading her, the black man has the power to love her back to life. This is accomplished through the divine function of breathing the life of unadulterated love into her physical, emotional and spiritual being. I believe in this with all of my soul.

Yes, there was a time when we were sold off from our families, not allowing us to bond with our progeny, nor did it allow us to ma-terialize covenantal commitment. Those impediments are gone, and it is time to recommit to loving our women through an action-based approach that provides her with the security and stability that allows her live optimally—functioning in the maximum capacity of her de-sign. This calls for the action of loving her from beyond our words. A place in which our words only serve to confirm what our actions have already expressed.

At first, it will be difficult, because it will call for you to elevate to a level that she may not be ready for. She may initially fight you and it may take a while, but she is designed to follow the man who knows how to lead her. It is important to understand that true leadership does not, in any way, involve dominance. When a man has found his spiritual center, and he has become aware of his identity and purpose, the confidence that is birthed allows him to lead his loved ones, especially his woman, with a sacrificial love that allows him to die to self, so that he may live for his purpose, which includes elevating her.

As the essence of his glory, she will reflect that unadulterated love in her countenance. When others look at her, they will be able to discern his character. This is powerful. This is the foundation of our future as a people.

Our children need us; however, we are limited in what we are able to give them until we are able to fully give each other what we need. Both, black men and black women are operating on fumes, with each possessing the power to reignite the passion and power in the other. It begins with men taking a position of absolute guardianship over our women.

If there is no struggle there is no progress.

Those who profess to favor freedom and yet deprecate agitation are men who want crops without plowing up the ground; they want rain without thunder and lightning. They want the ocean without the awful roar of its many waters.

Frederick Douglass
If There is No Struggle,
There is No Progress
1857

Chapter 11

The Conundrum
of the Black Struggle

There are two major issues that contribute to the perpetual state of oppression as far as black people are concerned.

1. We don't ask questions concerning how we developed our current thought patterns, or the way we process events that take place in our lives (e.g., Why we are so easy to forgive the most vile injustices against us?).

2. We don't seek answers for ourselves, but rather hope and wish for our oppressors to suddenly develop a conscience and then supply the relief we so desperately need.

The answer to the enigmatic conundrum, in which we find ourselves perpetually being oppressed and subjugated under, will not be solved by looking outward. This is an issue that must be solved from within. We must stop looking at the oppressor and demand that they respond, because they will not, since it is not in their best interest. Their very survival relies on their ability to oppress us.

We, and only we, possess the power and resources to lift ourselves up from the gutter of oppression. It starts with absolute economic empowerment achieved through the practice of black group economics. It is sustained through consistent education of our people that extends beyond the parameters of the attainment of academic skills.

To my Christian brothers and sisters, I am not here to issue condemnation or ridicule of your faith; but I am here to issue an indictment of your approach. Far too many of you are praying to God to deliver you from a giant that equipped you with the power to slay. You are talking, preaching and singing about faith, but you are failing to walk in it. Faith takes action; faith dares to be bold and step out of the confines of the status quo.

To my self-proclaimed conscious brothers and sisters, I am issuing an indictment of your approach. Far too many of you spend way too much time attacking those who don't believe what you believe and those who don't know what you think you know. Your energy would be better spent attacking the system that is oppressing and conditioning the minds of those you continually verbally assault. But then again, those people don't fight back, and the system does. Well, welcome to the war. I have been in this war for some time, fighting on a number of different fronts, and I have yet to see anyone converted from their views or beliefs due to verbal assaults from people with opposing views. In fact, the natural response in these instances is to hunker down and defend their beliefs.

So, then I have to question the motives of those that openly assault other blacks who don't see things their way. You can't really be about black empowerment, because you are spending more time attacking blacks than you are attacking the mechanisms of white supremacy. This means that your motives are self-serving as you personally stroke your own ego for knowing what amounts to very little in the scope of it all.

Black men, it is time to step from behind your narcissistic behavior in order to step up and step out to lead our people. It is time to stop the grandstanding and competing with one another. It is time for us to reengage the home in a manner that fortifies our presence and facilitates the complete development of our progeny.

Yes, we have created situations in which we have children in more than one household, by more than one woman; however, this must not stop us from developing a presence in each of those homes. No, we can't live in each one, but we must develop a presence in that home, and this presence must go beyond the paying of child support and weekly visits. It must extend to giving attention to the needs of that home, especially when there is no adult male presence in the home.

Contrary to popular belief and cultural paradigms, our responsibility to the mothers of our children does not stop with supporting our kids. The moment that we planted our seed within her womb, she became our family; therefore, she became our responsibility, subsequently making us responsible for her, until the point another man chooses to take her for his wife. This is true male responsibility. I know that this is not easy, because I live it every day; yet, it is what is required of the black man. We have abdicated our roles as leaders, protectors, coverings and providers, and now we must reclaim our roles.

Black women, you have systematically made the black man your enemy. The level of contempt and hostility that is consistently aimed at black men is remarkable. As you can see, I have not given the black man a pass. Yes, black men have abdicated their roles in the black collective. Many of them have found it to be an acceptable course of action to procreate and then abandon their progeny. There have been some who have found it to be within reason to be abusive towards you and others who have deemed it necessary to crush your dreams. For that, I personally I apologize, but now it is time to move forward.

It is time to realize that you are not without some culpability in the creation of the devastation of the black family nucleus. A long time ago, I wrote in my first book The Invisible Father: Reversing the Curse of a Fatherless Generation that behind every great black man is an equally great black woman. I iterated further that the reason that she is great is the fact that she is aware of his weaknesses and vulnerabilities, but instead of exposing them, she covers them—giving him the confidence to function in his strengths without having to be overly concerned about his weaknesses. No man wants a woman that exposes his weaknesses.

Far too many of our black sisters have deemed it necessary to expose the weaknesses and vulnerabilities of our black men, and then have the audacity to want to know why black men are pulling away. What you have considered to be your greatest strength is actually your greatest weakness.

There is nothing a man, regardless of race, despises more than disrespect and contempt. If you want to reach him, if you want to get his attention, that is not the way to do it. We black men need you by our side, if we are going to pick up the torch that has been lying dormant and quenched for some time now. We need your warmth and love. We need you to give spiritual birth to our visions and dreams after you have incubated them in the warmth of your spiritual womb. We need your love, encouragement and affirmation, because we were designed to respond to it.

And, we must all take on the responsibility of educating and empowering our youth. It is time to stop expecting a whitewashed Eurocentric education system to educate our children. We must take on the invaluable responsibility of providing our youth with their identity. Men, this begins with us. We are the source of identity, purpose and self-worth to our children. We are the model of masculinity and manhood to our male progeny, and we are the source of an elevated self-image for our daughters.

Our elevation begins with asking ourselves some tough questions about how and why, and it will be culminated through our response to the answers to those questions. No one else is going to come to our rescue because everyone else is benefitting from our demise. It is time to rise up and live at the level of our design!

Conclusion

When I was approached by the publisher to write this book, it was because they were aware of my passion and concern in this area. It is no secret that our children are our future. We must be willing to prepare them for what lies ahead of them. To be honest, to this point, we have not done a very good job. We have entrusted a European education system that is inherently hostile toward the creative capacity of our youth to educate and empower them. We have allowed education to be reduced to the acquisition of academic skills, while abandoning heritage and self-awareness.

It is our responsibility to educate our children holistically, moving beyond the exposure to academic disciplines into the realm of absolute empowerment. This means giving them everything that they need to successfully compete in their environment. It means introducing them to their true identity in a manner that eliminates the poison root of self-hatred and low self-esteem. It is about black parents standing up and doing what they were designed to do.

We must engage our children consistently, and it is our responsibility to monitor what enters into their perceptive gates. Not only must we guard against all the negativity that they are being bombarded with, but we must consistently disseminate positive information into their psyche. We have multitudinous mediums through which to do this. Instead of using social media as a platform for flirting and entertainment, it should be used as a teaching ground to empower the black race. We need to focus on starting our own propaganda campaign, since we have become so enamored with the one that white supremacy unleased on us.

The Black Community Empowerment Initiative is a program that I designed to go into inner-city communities to engage black youth for the purpose of passing on information, in a vast number of ways, in order to provide a comprehensive education that prepares them for what lies ahead. Instead of teaching them how to be employees in corporate America, we must give them a mindset that drives them toward ownership and entrepreneurship. We must remove the proclivity that we tend to have as a people to sell our ideas, creations and souls for cash, leaving us with nothing through which we can lift our people.

I am dedicated to being involved in the process at every level, and I hope that you will become committed as well.

IT IS TIME TO TAKE ACTION!

I believe that I have done a good job of illuminating the facts that educating our people, especially our youth, involves more that the academic disciplines that are taught in schools; but the learning of academics is still a vital aspect of the educational process.

With this in mind, we must take the time to evaluate the current state of the educational process for blacks in public schools.

1. In addition to the process of alienation and marginalization of black students who are in attendance at public schools, black students are expelled (not just suspended) at a rate three times the rate of white students.

2. One in four black boys with disabilities received an out-of-school suspension.

3. More than 25 percent of schools with a predominantly black population don't offer algebra II, and one third do not offer chemistry.

4. Black students account for 40 percent of enrollment in schools that offer gifted programs, but only represent 26 percent of the students enrolled in those programs.

5. Black schools have a significantly higher concentration of first-year teachers than white schools.

6. Blacks are three times more likely to attend schools in which the teachers are not adequately certified.

7. Black boys as young as five years old are consistently misdiagnosed with learning disorders, such as ADHD, and behavioral disorders, including oppositional defiant disorder, subsequently being prescribed psychotropic drugs, such as Zoloft, Ritalin, Vyvanse and more. Most of these drugs are classified as schedule-II drugs, meaning that they are highly addictive.

8. Young black males are automatically viewed as incapable of learning and having an exaggerated proclivity for behavioral problems.

Until we are able to build our own schools, we must take on the responsibility to educate our own children—initially in the form of homeschooling and community empowerment programs.

The Black Community Empowerment Initiative is the initial grassroots program designed to immediately introduce black youth to their identity through a holistic educational process. It is my goal to expand this model in order to take it on a national level. To learn more about the work that we are doing visit http://www.theodyssey-project21.com. This battle will not be won by sitting on the sidelines hoping for a brighter tomorrow. It will come by empowering ourselves and our progeny to be prepared to seize every opportunity for advancement. So, let each of us stand up and step out.

THE CRY OF A BLACK NATION

As a race, blacks have come to a crossroads—a place in time in which a decision must be made. In a nation, such as America, where millions of immigrants fight to find refuge so that they may pursue dreams associated with this nation's heritage, we as a people still struggle to find our footing in the country that the blood and sweat of our ancestors built. What can be even more frustrating is the fact that our people seem to be caught up in the vortex of desolation and despair.

We are facing some prodigious challenges as a collective people. Young black males are dropping out of high school at rates as high as 75 out of every 100 in some metropolitan areas. Young black girls are three times more likely to become pregnant before they graduate high school than their white counterparts. To exacerbate matters, in comparison to 1969 when more than 75 percent of all black couples were married and remained together, blacks have the highest divorce rate out of all major ethnic groups in America—with a current divorce rate of 48 percent.

It is clear that the black family nucleus has been systematically decimated by a system that has been perpetuated against it for centuries. From the days of slavery when the black man was forced to breed and then sold away from his wife and progeny to the ruling by the federal government in the 1960s that stated that no federal subsidies would be provided to households in which an able-bodied male resided. This was during a time when many black men found it extremely difficult to find steady employment or to find employment that would provide a sufficient income to support their families.

I consistently work with inner-city children who are part of communities in which there is a 95 percent or higher female head of household ratio. This means that the children in these communities are being robbed of the vital nurturing and support that is inherent with a two-parent household.

REWRITING THE BLACK NARRATIVE OUR WAY

Over the last several years there have been a number of my contemporaries that have been able to lucidly and effectively communicate the black narrative and what that means for blacks in America. I strongly believe that the communication of this narrative is extremely important to the process of developing strategies that can be implemented and executed successfully. What concerns me is that far too many of our leaders seem to be satisfied with simply presenting their perspective of the black narrative. They have become quite astute at telling our story and presenting our reality; however, what seems to be lacking is the development of plans and strategies that will facilitate black elevation and empowerment.

The black struggle is significantly more than a discussion of issues and the assessment of blame. I agree that the narrative must be made clear to the masses. I am not very interested in presenting the black narrative to whites as a collective, because I don't believe in the quest to recruit the help of whites or other non-blacks for the purpose of assisting blacks in our fight for empowerment. I believe that it is counterproductive in a number of ways. I believe that it is extremely important for blacks to come together to build and develop our economic system through which elevation and empowerment will emerge.

It is time for blacks to relinquish their perpetual quest to assimilate into a system that has been perpetually hostile toward us. It is time for blacks to abandon the need and desire to earn the approbation and validation of whites. This means that before we can topple the mountain of white supremacy, we must exorcise our own demons. We must learn to appreciate and embrace our own brilliance. We must come to the understanding that rewriting the black narrative our way is essential to true empowerment. Empowerment begins as a state of mind that acknowledges the power and gifts within.

WHITE SUPREMACY AS A CONCEPT AND NOT A REALITY

There has been an ever increasing cognizance of white supremacy and the impact that it has had on the black narrative. Those who have taken the time to study this institution of white racism are keenly cognizant of the innumerable machinations through which this system of power systematically oppresses the black race. Once again, I believe that it is important for blacks to understand how white supremacy functions in their everyday world. Most blacks don't have a lucid understanding of racism. They tend to view racism as individual snapshots of bigotry-driven incidents, rather than seeing the entire cohesive institutionalized system that virtually functions on auto pilot.

Racism isn't the act of a white supervisor showing favor to a white subordinate over a more qualified black one. Racism is the system of power in place that facilitates that type of behavior. In fact, racism rewards that type of behavior.

While acknowledging the existence of racism, it is important not to give this system absolute power or read more into its title than you should. White supremacy is an internal concept, it is not the reality of the world. In other words, white people are not supreme and neither are they superior in any way. The thought of supremacy is their internal concept and it explains their actions and focus—it is the definition of the aggregate expectation of the sum total of every machination it perpetuates. It is their method of fighting for dominance and the perpetuation of their race. What blacks must understand is that it is our compliance that affords white supremacy its power. Without black compliance, white supremacy means absolutely nothing. This is the message that must become clear to blacks as a collective. For far too long, blacks have bought into the myth that compliance and assimilation would bring about peace and harmony. The truth is that the black race represents the potential extermination of the white race, so absolute peace between mortal enemies is not a realistic expectation. The only way that we will experience peace is through power. We must possess the power to protect our interests. We must possess the power to potentially retaliate to any negative actions perpetuated against us.

After we finally realize that white supremacy has no power that we don't give it, we will begin to invest that power in ourselves. We will begin to share the image of a race of people with unlimited potential. We will begin to rewrite our narrative through the lens of a paradigm that is reflective of our absolute greatness and our royal bloodlines. When we begin to tell our own story through our own perspective, we will begin to experience the power that is associated with the connection with our authentic identity. It is in finding this identity that we will uncover our purpose, and it is our purpose that will fuel our passion and drive toward the absolute greatness that is in our destiny.

We must learn to be unapologetic about our love of and for ourselves. We must never become consumed with concern about how our self-love may offend others. Once we learn to love ourselves, we will actually discover that the love we thought we were extending to other groups was not love at all, but a plea for validation and acceptance. You see, you can never truly love anyone else until you have developed an authentic love for yourself. As long as you think your skin is too dark, or your nose is too wide, you still have not learned to love yourself. You must learn to love who you are without fault.

Once self-love has entered the equation, there will be a natural yearning for something better. Authentic love, especially self-love, demands the best. The reason that the vast majority of blacks have taken no decisive action to elevate themselves is that self-hatred has convinced them that they are not worthy of it. Self-love demands the best from within.

Self-love will demand that you work with others who look like you for the betterment of the collective. It will allow you to begin the process of writing a new narrative—a narrative of power, elevation and progression. Rewriting the black narrative our way, seizes the power of self-reliance and self-awareness, and it releases blacks from the need to be validated or accepted by any other group. Rewriting our narrative unleashes us from the shackles of psychological bondage and the feelings of inferiority, and it plants us firmly on the platform of exceptional greatness.

THE IFS SYNDROME

When I wrote *The Invisible Father: Reversing the Curse of a Fatherless Generation* more than eight years ago, I engaged a systematic epidemic that I called IFS—The Invisible Father Syndrome. IFS encompasses the collective results that are consequential to the black father being absent in the home. In a home in which the father is not present, the male child is more likely to assimilate effeminate characteristics from the present mother, and female children will develop a negative image of the black male which will fuel their contempt for him. The female progeny will also lack a sense of identity and self-worth as these qualities are inextricably intertwined to the direct relationship between father and daughter.

As these developmental issues go unaddressed, the female becomes more promiscuous as she begins to search for the love and confirmation that she never received from her father. The young male finds himself on a lonely island of dysfunctional paradigms through which he attempts to make sense of what he perceives to be his own manhood. Because he has not had any concrete examples by which to set a standard, he looks outside the home for validation and acceptance. Meanwhile, he lives in an oblivious state, in which he is totally unaware of the system that has been designed to capitalize on his developmental deficiencies. He has heard about or maybe even read the statistics that point to the fact that he is more likely to go to prison than to college; yet he does not have the coherent capacity associated with a mature and developed psyche to fully elucidate the meaning of those numbers. There is a good possibility that he has bought into the lie that the struggle is simply his lot in life.

This is the movie that continues to play over and over in the lives of far too many black children in this nation. We, as a people, must come together in solidarity to confront these issues. I was speaking with one of the female members of The Odyssey Project and she said something to me that was succinct, yet extremely profound. With great sincerity, she said, "the time is up for pointing the finger of blame. Men need to man up and women need to fall in behind our men." Her assessment was not only right, but it stands as the primary imperative to what has to happen for us to elevate ourselves in an aggregate manner.

As the blood of our young men continues to flow into the streets of inner-city neighborhoods, I can hear the cry of our people—a black nation—as we yearn for justice. I can hear the cry of our women as they plead for true male leadership. I can hear the cry of our young daughters as their hearts beg for the purity of their father's love and assurance of who they are. I can hear the cries of our young men as they resist the seemingly implacable force of conformity to a white racist system. I see their sagging pants as a last ditch effort to resist total consumption by a foreign non-culture.

The time has come to rise up to face our destiny. We have built wealth for all others except ourselves. We have labored while the white man has amassed wealth and power through the sweat of our brow. It is now our turn to build wealth and power. It is now our turn to stand strong and bold. It is now our turn to raise our heads in ultimate confidence of who we are and where we come from. We come from the stock of kings and queens. There is royalty coursing through our veins. Even the dances that we have been taught and conditioned to believe are ratchet—whatever that means—are actually ancient cultural dances that are still celebrated by our brothers and sisters in Africa.

Our children need us to stand on their behalf. They need us to be invested in their futures. It is imperative that we offer them more than what has been offered to us. It is vital that we give them an opportunity to walk from underneath the cloud of depression and oppression that makes it hard for them to breathe. It is time to rise. It is time to shake off the dust of ignorance and the residue of subservience to put on the cloak of aristocracy and royalty. It is time to lay down the veil of self-hatred so that we may slip on the armor of Kings and the adornment of Queens. It is time to stare down our destiny with an inexorable passion to overcome. To all my beautiful sisters and powerful brothers, I simply say: "THE TIME IS NOW!"

Bibliography

Akbar, Dr. Na'im. *Breaking the Chains of Psychological Slavery*. Mind Productions Publications, 1996.

Alexander, Michelle. *The New Jim Crow: Mass Incarceration in the Age of Color Blindness*. The New Press, 2010.

Anderson, Claud. *Black Labor, White Wealth: The Search for Power and Economic Justice*. Powernomics Corporation of America, 1994.

Bertrand, Marianne. *Racial Bias in Hiring*. University of Chicago School of Business, 2003.

Burrell, Tom. *Brainwashed: Challenging the Myth of Black Inferiority*. Smiley Books, 2010.

Codrington, Jamila, and Fairchild, Halford H. *Special Education and the Mis-education of African American Children*. Association of Black Psychologists, 2012.

Cohen, Patricia. *For Recent Black College Graduates, a Tougher Road to Employment*. New York Times, 2014.

Cress-Welsing, Francis. *The Cress Theory of Color Confrontation*, C-R Publishers, 1989.

DeGruy, Joy. *Post Traumatic Slave Syndrome*. Joy DeGruy Publications Inc, 2005.

Deluzain, H. Edward. *Names and Personality*. Behind the Name, 1996.

Desilver, Drew. *Black Unemployment Rate is Consistently Twice that of Whites*. Fact Tank, 2013.

Douglass, Frederick. *If There is No Struggle, There is No Progress*. 1857.

Flatow, Nicole. "The United States Has The Largest Prison Population in the World—and It's Growing," *Thing Progess.org*. 2014.

Green, Tanya L. "The Negro Project: Margaret Sanger's Eugenic Plan for Black America," *BackGenocide.org*. 2012.

Hare, Nathan and Hare, Julia. "The Role of the Black Male in Today's Society," *The Black Think Tank*. 2014.

Johnson, Dr. Umar. *Black Compliance is Not the Answer to White Supremacy*. The Odyssey Consortium, 2014.

Kristof, Nicholas. "Fact Check: Grim Statistics on Race and Police Killings," *CNN*. 2014.

Malthus, Thomas Robert. *Principle of Population*. Oxford University Press, 1798.

Martinez, Elizabeth. "What is White Supremacy?," *SOA Watch*. 2015.

Mattison, R.E. *Use of Psychotropic Medications in Special Education Students with Serious Emotional Disturbance*. National Institute of Health, 1999.

McCormack, Simon. "Black Men Who Dropped Out of High School Have Very High Risk of Going to Prison: Study," *Huffington Post*. 2014.

Murdock, Sebastian. "Darrin Manning, Pa. Teen, Allegedly Has Testicle Ruptured by Cop," *Huffington Post*. 2014.

Sanger, Margaret. *Woman, Morality, and Birth Control*. New York Publishing Company, 1922.

Stapp, Katherine. *Black Children Often Mislabeled as Hyperactive in the United States*. 2014.

"Statistics of Incarcerated African American Males." Wikipedia.

Thieme, R.B. *Daniel: Chapters One Through Six*. R.B. Thieme Ministries, 1996.

Toldson, Ivory A. "Think You Know the Dropout Rates for Black Males? You're Probably Wrong," *The Root*. 2014.

Wallace, Rick. *The Self-affirming Force of a Christian Self-image*. Straight From the Lab, 2014.

Woodson, Carter G. *The Mis-Education of the Negro*,. Tribeca Books, 1933.

Younge, Gary. "The Routine Criminalization of Young Black Men is a Nation's Shame," *Alternet*. 2014.

About Rick Wallace

Dr. Rick Wallace (Ph.D.) is a champion of the cause of black men reclaiming their positions as leaders, protectors, providers, and coverings for their families and others. He also believes that the confusion of male and female roles in the black community has further exacerbated the schismatic issues that continue to drive the black man and the black woman apart—consequently devastating the black family nucleus. While he knows about the fallible nature of the woman, he focuses his primary efforts on encouraging and empowering young black men to take the lead, believing that most black women will adjust by nature. Dr. Wallace also places immense significance on the holistic education of black youth, asserting that not only has the public education system mis-educated and underprepared black youth for the competitive world in which they must reside, but black parents and the black community have also failed in the task of holistically educating youths beyond the acquisition of academic skills.

Dr. Wallace is a creative and talented author. He published his first article in 1985 ("The Invisible Father"), at the age of 17, and has been writing ever since. That original article eventually became the inspiration for his first book: *The Invisible Father: Reversing the Curse of a Fatherless Generation.* He has since authored 15 other books such as: *Abiding in Abundance, Renewing Your Mind: The Dynamics of Christian Transformation, When Your House Is Not a Home,* and his latest contribution, *The Mis-education of Black Youth in America.* Additionally, Dr. Wallace has published two doctoral dissertations that include "The Influence of Theocratic Concepts on Social Culture" and his latest contribution, "The Influence of Cognitive Distortions on the Social Mobility" and "Mental Health of African Americans." He believes in holistically addressing issues rather than applying social Band-Aids to the horrific wound of the black collective.

CPSIA information can be obtained
at www.ICGtesting.com
Printed in the USA
BVOW07s0739120218
507487BV00005B/108/P

9 780989 830430